For Margot Lamont Heap
and
David

in hopes you will enjoy
this family read!

Loving

North Haven
July 1999

No Twilight About Me

A Life in Letters

Florence Corliss Lamont • Thomas William Lamont
Canterbury Cathedral, England

No Twilight About Me

A Life in Letters

Lansing Lamont

Strawtown Press
New York

Printed in the United States of America
ISBN 0-9665542-1-3
First Edition
Strawtown Press
New York

To the Clan
Past, Present and Forever

"When I die, Tommy dear, do not visit my grave Christmas day. I shall not be in it, but somewhere round the Christmas tree, or where the fun is—that's where you will find me."

—Florence Corliss Lamont
to her eldest son,
December 28, 1921

Foreword

Once upon a golden time in a faraway age, my grandparents and a handful of their peers were the closest thing in America to royalty.

They were lodestars in a not yet weightless society that still esteemed the virtues of accountability, forthrightness and refinement. Theirs was not the tinseled royalty of Palm Beach, Hollywood or Newport, but royalty earned through serious endeavor of a high order. My grandfather earned it in the service of commanding international causes. My grandmother earned it through tireless energy devoted to cultural and educational good works.

He was the last great banker of the Diplomatic Age, the most resourceful and compleat of the Morgan partners, the man who adroitly managed the financial affairs of troubled nations and magnified the lustre of his bank by doing so. She was the partnership's intellectual conscience, its moral uplift. In a world run by practical, self-interested men of affairs he was the master of his game, cited often as the most influential man in America, the banker-internuncio without peer. She adorned his world with scholarship, idealism and vivacity. Thomas William Lamont, Florence Corliss Lamont. Good King Tom and Queen Florence. TWL. FCL.

They burnished their times. They reigned with benevolence, charm and politesse. Together, in the three decades after the first World War, they cut a grand swath.

TWL had started out as a newspaperman, a financial reporter, but shortly switched to a career in finance, the better to support his growing family. It was he who guided J.P. Morgan's bank to new heights through momentous political and diplomatic crises, earning kudos from the world press and business community.

FCL met the challenges of fame, motherhood and social ascent with unblinking equipoise. She would upbraid a right-wing Congressman with the same stinging intensity she used on her defiantly leftish second son. Her children and celebrated dinner guests were treated equally to the same overcooked meals and no-nonsense conversation, all in butlered splendor. Dullards weren't asked back to high table.

They were feted at home and abroad. FCL, who'd earned a graduate degree in philosophy from Columbia, teaed and crumpeted with the literary set. TWL settled for private audiences with kings, presidents and prime ministers. Neither of them took their celebrity too seriously. Grandpa never forgot his roots in a humble Methodist parsonage in upstate New York. Grandma was too enthralled with God and saving the souls of her children to bask in the limelight. Large parties and other pointless frolics wearied her. She would rather play games with her grandchildren or lecture an errant clergyman.

Publicly, FCL and TWL wore the responsibilities of fame and wealth with a gravitas that reflected the dominant institutions in their lives: Harvard, Smith College, the House of Morgan, the Presbyterian church. As a youth, reading the news stories about them, I thought them a dauntingly earnest and high-minded couple. Nothing in my childhood experience altered that impression—neither the formal Sunday luncheons at their weekend manse, where the china rattled to heated arguments over the Fate of Man, or the summer picnics on a Maine island where FCL read Wordsworth aloud while enthroned amidst the granite rocks.

Only many decades later, having rediscovered a long-forgotten cache of letters from FCL and TWL to their four children, did I begin to fathom how their extraordinary lives had meshed such a dog's dish of domestic pickles and parental stews with such a store of unbridled romanticism and extravagance.

Their wardrobes could have filled entire floors at Harrods or Triplers. FCL had more hats than Hedda Hopper; she also had a flair for rapturous prose that would have dazzled the Hollywood gossip queen and done the Bronte sisters proud. TWL spiffed up his banker's image with silk pajamas and striped waistcoats; he sported them preferably aboard his yacht while steaming up the Hudson or across Long Island sound. Their travels abroad resembled the processionals of the early Khans.

In private, though, they were a vulnerable pair in the most prosaic sense. They may have marched staunchly self-assured across the pages of the New York *Times* or the *Herald Tribune,* at ease in the company of poets and statesmen. But within the walls of their various domiciles they were as putty when confronted with wayward children or temperamental servants. The simplest household appliances defied them. They were prisoners to the everyday frustrations of broken plumbing, electrical short-circuits, indulgent house guests. They wrestled with the same anxieties of other parents about the character and discipline of their exuberant offspring.

Their normally ordered lives seemed able to accommodate the wildest swerves of comic mayhem. They seemed perpetually floundering in Thurberish befuddlement over some child's errancy. The sensible pieties they sought to instil in their young were constantly being derailed by fits of outrage at some unforeseen blasphemy—a cook on the bottle, a motor car in extremis, a vacation ruined by termites. That it all transpired at a rarified level made it no less flummoxing. Their regal style was no guarantee against intrusions by addled relatives, titled bores, old-boy panhandlers and the inebriates of this world. The vagaries of unruly youth, not to mention English weather, frequently undid their best-laid plans.

Over time, as world events assumed ever greater urgency, their chatty free-flowing letters assumed a darker, more reflective tone. They continued to rail at their hapless small defeats in the technological age and to chide their grown children on matters of deportment and health, physical and spiritual. To his oldest banker son, TWL wrote of hard practical matters: what worked and didn't work in the complex worlds of international politics and finance, the realities of compromise. To her atheistic, socialist-leaning, irrepressible second son, FCL covered the pages with passionate pleas that he foreswear his Godless ways. But, increasingly, the outpourings of fervor for shining ideals and principles gave way to musings on war and death, on the eternal quest for peace. More frequently, the parents aired sharp differences of opinion between themselves, or with their children, on pressing issues of public policy.

It may be unfair to judge, a half-century later, the political correctness of some of the anecdotes and observations in these letters, reflecting the mindset of privilege and class in those times. They sound at once quaint, possibly antediluvian, but also refreshing. These days we have become so socially sensitized, so politically circumspect, we've waived the kind of unvarnished candor and spontaneity these letters convey. If they occasionally strike a condescending note, the lapse is probably FCL's, and probably advertent. Grandma was seldom tentative or mealy-mouthed. She would never call a spade a digging implement.

From the first exchange of letters in the fall of 1913 to FCL's last note in the spring of 1952, the correspondence spanned nearly four decades—a kaleidoscopic time that included two World Wars, the Gilded Age of plutocracy, the Crash of 1929, the Depression, and the transforming New Deal years. In the midst of it all, FCL and TWL nurtured their own special oasis which these letters trace. They offer, as their original collator observed, the "delight in being for awhile in the company of two remarkable people and their family, two parents, spirited and spiritual, who embraced life eagerly and embraced it whole, and who took time out from busy days to share their adventures with those who were closest to them".

There is here much that is wise, occasionally profound, for the writers were thoughtful missionary people. Yet they leavened their manna with the fizziest of gossip and skinning observation. The core of wisdom they imparted to their children was enveloped by warmth and wit and an ever faithful regard for life's brimming hopes and expectations. Edited for that focus, these letters, many in abridged or excerpted form, portray a familial vignette of life at the top in the first half of this century.

L.L.
New York, N.Y.
June 1999

The Family

TWL	—	Thomas William Lamont, father
FCL	—	Florence Corliss Lamont, mother
TSL	—	Thomas Stilwell Lamont, first son
CL	—	Corliss Lamont, second son
AL	—	Austin Lamont, third son
EAL/ELC	—	Eleanor Allen Lamont/Eleanor Lamont Cunningham, daughter and fourth child

TWL (1870-1948).

Son of Scots-descended Methodist pastor. Had read Bible twice by time he was 14. Worked his way on scholarships through preparatory school and college (Harvard '92), tutoring other students for pay. Convivial, urbane, tolerant to a fault. Eternal optimist, slow to anger, humane and patient in his dealings. Possessed the healing touch, the gift of being able to imbue thorniest dispute or darkest doubter with the logic and warmth of his person. Sound, if not prescient. Tenderly wise. Relished a good laugh. Generous of heart and purse. Was, in the words of one of his children, "Father, creator of us all, and, like God, sometimes astonished at the results."

FCL (1872-1952).

Ivy Orator, Smith College, class of '93. Resolute, intellectually ambitious, intolerant of the petty and mundane. Also ardent, quirky, capricious, addicted to the spiritual, the philosophic. The title of her Columbia University master's thesis: "A Criticism of Browning's Dramas from the Aristotelian Point of View". Wary of contraptions and things. Believed deeply, fiercely defended her beliefs. Ungladly suffered fools and second raters. Oblivious to popular icons like film stars and sports heroes (claimed never to have heard of Babe Ruth). Could bag a stuffed shirt at fifty yards with one well-aimed epistolary barb. Quest for perfection gave her on occasion what one writer described as "a bluestocking intensity." Not to be trifled with.

TSL (1899-1967).

His father's son. Slight of build, strong of voice. Sensible, virtuous, diligent. At age 11 edited Englewood (N.J.) News, three-page weekly which retailed for 3¢ a copy, yearly subscription price 55¢. Week of March 23, 1910, paper reported, "Editor lost all his copies of Englewood News for week of January 19. Would be very thankful if someone would lend him a copy." Gave up journalism for banking. Rose to vice-chairman of Morgan Guaranty Trust, his father's mutated old bank. Served abroad with U.S. Eighth Air Force during World War II. Considered more conventional and proper than his high-flying father. Sired four children. Answered to the name of Tommy.

CL (1902-1995).

His mother's son. Headstrong, high-spirited, charged with intellectual energy. Fiercely unconventional, possessed of early rebellious streak. Started raising hell at prep school and college, never stopped. Protested student restrictions at Exeter Academy, labor policies at Harvard, capitalist policies on Wall Street, foreign policies of U.S. Government. Anti-war activist. Ran for political office on Socialist-

Labor ticket, regularly defeated. Regularly denied being a Communist. Full-blown atheist and practicing humanist. Championed Soviet Union, human rights, 1st Amendment freedoms. Challenged Sen. Joseph McCarthy, and won. Defiant, quixotic, exasperating. Family loyalist and archivist. Four children.

AL (1905-1969).

Had father's charm, mother's coltishness. Unlike CL, preferred scaling social heights at college rather than barricades. Occasionally distracted parents with escapades. After postgraduate studies at Oxford, entered medicine. Practiced in Baltimore, then Philadelphia, becoming a much respected anesthesiologist. Polished, good-looking, at times austere. Married well, and twice. Four children.

EAL/ELC (1910-1961).

Came of age in Roaring Twenties. Precocious, irrepressible. Object of doting, thoroughly perplexed parents. Carried flapper instincts, blithe spirit to Milton Academy in Boston, Smith College, and into marriage to dashing Harvard graduate who became one of nation's prominent arts administrators. Bright, fizzy, popular belle of Hartford, Connecticut. Four children.

TWL's and FCL's children, ca. 1914.
Left to right, CL, EL, TSL and AL.

The Family Homes

Englewood, New Jersey	(ca. 1895-1920)
New York City, N.Y.	(1921-1952)
Palisades, New York	(weekends, 1928-1950)
North Haven, Maine	(summers, 1919-1952)

In the fall of 1913, TWL's and FCL's oldest son TSL entered Phillips Exeter Academy in New Hampshire. Six months earlier, the elder J. Pierpont Morgan had died. His son J.P. Morgan Jr. had taken over the bank where TWL, now 43, had been a partner for the past two years. The family correspondence began in earnest that September. While the bulk of the letters are overwhelmingly one-way, from TWL and FCL to their children, the earliest ones came from their older boys away for the first time from home.

TSL to FCL
Exeter, September 1913

Dear Mother

It has been pouring rain ever since you left. If you want to get me something for Xmas, get me a chair that turns around like Grandpa's and has a soft seat like his. I have to sit for hours on a very hard wood seat. All the boys have Grandpa's kind. And not a boy in school wears rubbers no matter how muddy or wet the streets are. Love to all. Tommy.

TSL to TWL
Exeter, September 1913

Dear Father,

I think Exeter is a wonderful place. Only it is mighty punk of it not to have licked Andover[1] since 1905. Hasn't even tied with it. Last night I went to the reception given by the Senior Council for the new

---

[1] Phillips Andover Academy was Exeter's main rival.

kids. T.A.D. Jones, the football coach, spoke[1]. Jones worked himself up to a pitch where the tears streamed down his face, his voice caught, and he nearly broke down. He told how the old grads had picked up their morning papers for years now and hadn't read of how Exeter had won . . .

FCL to TSL
New York City, October 1913

We are both concerned about your failure to get regular exercise. The other boys get exercise, and I should think that when the weather is decent you could play tennis . . .

TSL to FCL
Exeter, October 22, 1913

Dear Mother,
Nobody in school plays tennis for the simple reason that it can't be played under a foot of water. It has rained almost every day since September 17 . . .

TWL to TSL
New York City, February 14, 1914

Your letter to your mother, which came yesterday, did not scare her. It simply made her sad to think that she had a son who had reached his sixteenth year and yet had so little discretion. If a man or boy were dead sure of being able to keep in perfect condition and never pick up a germ, then very likely he could toughen himself so he could get his feet wet without fear, and sleep in icy blasts, etc. The difficulty is that nobody can keep in perfect condition, and the moment you get a little run down or tired, get your feet wet or anything like that, there is the deuce to pay. When I was at Exeter, one of my young friends who thought he could toughen himself this way

[1] Ten years later, in the fall of 1923, Jones, by then head football coach at Yale, gained immortality with these words to the varsity squad on the day of The Game: "Gentlemen, you're now going out to play football against Harvard. Never again in your whole life will you do anything so important."

toughened himself into a case of pneumonia. Another one picked up tuberculosis and died within a year. So it pays to be careful . . .

TSL to TWL
Exeter, February 1915

Dear Father,

I don't see why you should suddenly become so wrought up just because I happen to flunk two hours. You evidently have a very wrong idea about flunking. The Upper Middle year is the hardest in school. It is not an important or a bad thing to flunk two hours of math for one month. I am doing my lessons up as brown as I ever expect to, and that's as brown as I can do. I wish you would communicate with Mr. Chase. If you hear from him that I am not doing very well in my studies, I'll drop something. I'll resign from the Exonian[1], the Musical Clubs and all other interests, and buy some glasses with heavy lenses and keep my door locked all the time.

The following year the Lamonts' second son CL, aged 14, entered Exeter. He was housed in Dunbar Hall, a campus dormitory run by a housemaster named Webber.

CL to FCL
Exeter, N.H., September 1916

This is certainly a rotten place to live in and I wouldn't room here another year for anything. There are so many restrictions. I would like to know why you got me a room opposite Mr. Webber. I can't have any fun. You can't make any kind of noise. I can't even play my victrola without Webber coming in and making me shut all my doors and windows so it gets awfully stuffy. You knew that if you put me in this room I could never have any fun or rough-house. It may have

[1]The Exonian, the student newspaper.

some bearing on my whole school life. No boys ever want to call on me here.

Some day I am going to have a good time and a good rough-house despite Mr. Webber, and will probably get punished for it. If I go out of my room after 8 p.m., I am bound to get caught, while if I was down the hall I could do it without getting caught, and I am going to do it some night, too.

I suppose you thought the old boy would have a good influence on me or some such thing. But I tell you, mother, it is the worst thing you could do for me because the more restrictions I have, the more I want to do the restricted things. And as there's no *reason* why I shouldn't do what all the other boys here do, I am going to do it, Webber or no Webber.

I am very mad now, so I had better stop and let myself cool down.

Your loving
Corliss

It was the last days of innocence, the years before America's entry into World War I. It was a carefree time, the air soft and easy, when school boys could still get worked up over dorm rules and parents still carried on at length over their children's health habits. TWL was now a Harvard Overseer and a Morgan partner of growing distinction. He was used to being accorded certain amenities, although his second son hotly disapproved.

TWL to TSL
Dark Harbor, Maine, October 18, 1916

Dear Tommy,

Last Friday evening I started up for Dark Harbor in a private car that I had borrowed from the New York Central people[1], leaving

[1] The New York Central Railroad.

New York at half past seven. After I had my solitary dinner on the car, I was reading some important papers when all of a sudden a tall, disheveled young man rushed in, looking wildly around and demanding to know if I was a physician. I said I wasn't, but asked what I could do for him. He said, "I think I am dying, just put your hand on my heart." (ed. It seems that in addition to having a suspect heart, the youth had been drinking heavily before boarding the train. After TWL assured him he wasn't dying, they introduced themselves).

"Are you any relation to Tommy Lamont?" the youth asked. I owned up to being the proud father. "Well," he said, "don't you remember me at Quogue? My name is Julian Sloan. Tommy's little brother Corliss hit me over the head with a croquet mallet, and Mrs. Lamont thought I was killed. I finished Yale last year and am on my way back to see a football game."

I woke up in Portland to find myself an hour and a half late with all connections missed. The railroad people were very kind, however, and made up a special little train to run me a hundred miles or so up to Burnham Junction. They telephoned ahead to have a motor car meet me there and take me down to Belfast . . .

Love,
Father

CL to FCL
Exeter, November 13, 1916

Dear Mother,

I heard yesterday from Tommy that you were coming up to see the Andover game and am very pleased that you are. Only I don't like the idea of you coming up in a private car, and will absolutely refuse to go anywhere near it. If it was known that my parents and myself had a private car everywhere they went, I would probably be called "Private-Car Lamont" forever after . . .

Affectionately,
Corliss

By 1917, the war in Europe was edging closer to America. TSL was in his last term at Exeter, preparing for Harvard. TWL found himself trying to temper his oldest boy's patriotic fervor as well as his overwrought criticism of the Morgan bank's role in the war effort. Early that year Germany declared its intent to conduct unrestricted submarine warfare in retaliation for America's and other non-combatants' ships ferrying supplies across the Atlantic to the Allies.

TWL to TSL
New York City, February 5, 1917

. . . There is not nearly as much excitement here as you might think. We are marking time, waiting for developments. Even if we get into actual war with Germany, it will take a year and a half to get any sort of an army into training. The great lack is not men but officers to train the men. Of course, before a year and a half is over, the war will be ended or I shall be greatly mistaken.

TSL to TWL
Exeter, March 1917

I suppose Corliss wrote you how he was caught pinning a "Silent Menace" sign on Mr. Webber's door. (ed. German submarines were known as the Silent Menace). He came very near getting in serious trouble for that. Tell him not to be such a kid and not to sing so horribly loud in chapel. He roars the hymns . . .

CL on Exeter Academy hocky team, 1920.

The war was still distant from TSL's student life, his concerns about his younger brother, the parlous financial state of his campus fraternity. He blamed the latter crisis on inflation and, by extension, his father's bank.

TSL to TWL
Exeter, March 1917

. . . It's all due to the high cost of living. You don't realize what sugar at 30¢ a pound means to some people. You New Yorkers and those connected with munitions and the buying of munitions are making such a lot of money. I think Morgan & Co. ought to set aside a few of the millions they are making to conduct an investigation into the high price of food and have some of these big food magnates arrested. The goodwill earned would more than offset the money lost. I wouldn't blame a person a single bit for setting off a bomb under your office as things are nowadays . . .

As early as 1914, J.P. Morgan & Co. had taken the lead in organizing loans and lines of credit to expedite Allied purchases of war supplies, including munitions, in the United States. By early 1917 TWL was the Morgan partner with major responsibility in this field. After offering to help with whatever monies might be needed for TSL's fraternity, he ended his response to TSL as follows:

TWL to TSL
New York City, March 8, 1917

. . . I think perhaps you are inclined to criticize pretty freely without actually knowing very many facts upon which to base your criticisms. It is all right to deplore conditions, and I am very happy to have you sympathize with and concerned for people who are playing hard luck. It is an awfully good sign and I hope you will never change in that respect. But please remember that it is just not right to criticize people unless you have the facts to indicate that they are responsible for the deplorable conditions in question.

On Good Friday, April 6, 1917 President Woodrow Wilson formally declared war on Germany. Nothing in their lives had prepared TWL and FCL and their children for the violent times ahead, for the radical changes in the human condition that would take place. Across the country military training camps were being set up. By the end of April, with informal training already underway at Exeter, TSL was writing his parents about the prospect of attending one of the summer training camps being organized for boys his age.

TWL to TSL
New York City, May 18, 1917

In regard to your anxiety to do some work for your country this summer, I too have learned that the training camps for boys your age are either to be abolished entirely or are to be run without regular army officers, so they will be no good to attend. But I am happy to tell you that Mr. Davison[1] has offered to take you on his personal staff in connection with the big Red Cross work. He will make his headquarters in Washington and plans to take a house there. You would be his personal aide. That sounds rather grand and I suppose it means errand boy . . . This strikes me as a wonderful plan, giving you an insight into organization and business methods, a chance to see how Mr. Davison does things in a large way, getting you somewhat in touch with what is going on in Washington and with the

[1]Henry P. Davison, a senior Morgan partner, close friend and colleague of TWL.

people there, at the same time putting you in a position that you may feel you are doing your little bit this summer for the Cause.

The plan worked to everyone's satisfaction. It may have been the sum of TSL's only protracted experience in Washington. In years to come he preferred to limit his visits there. Meanwhile, he was off to Harvard that fall.

TWL to Professor Greenough, Department of English, Harvard
New York City, September 21, 1917

I have expressed to Tom the hope that he would select as his major subject in college, English, not that he has any very great aptitude for writing . . . but because from my own experience I was convinced that a fair proficiency in English would best serve him in his after life (ed. sic).

Yours sincerely,

That fall TWL joined a presidential mission to England and France, headed by President Wilson's top adviser, Colonel Edward House. While there, TWL toured the British front.

TWL to TSL
New York City, November 3, 1917

Your mother feels dreadfully over the trip I am taking. I shall be back safe and sound for Christmas, I trust, and shall feel that I have tried to do a little something more in the war. If there should ever be any accident, your first duty would be to care for your mother. You will not have to support her, but love and cherish and keep her. She is the most wonderful mate, the most devoted mother.

TSL at Harvard

A year later, the war was sputtering to a close, the armistice imminent. TWL was the proud owner of the New York Evening Post, the paper his late brother Hammond had served as managing editor. TWL's youngest son Austin had left home to spend the year at Pomfret, a prep school in Connecticut, enroute to Exeter.

FCL to AL
New York City, Fall 1918

Precious love,

I just hated to go and leave you yesterday afternoon. I shall be awfully interested to get a letter from you telling me everything—how the football goes, whether your feet hurt when you left your arches off, how your lessons go, *everything.*

I reached home late and tired. Father met me and told me that Corliss had telegraphed that he was coming home and that Eleanor (ed. EAL) had a sore throat, a high fever and a stomach ache. No rest for the weary! I rushed home, woke Eleanor up about 11 o'clock, and it took the combined efforts of the entire family, father included, to get a dose of castor oil down her reluctant throat. She is lots better this morning and Dr. Lansing does not think it is going to amount to anything. So I feel better.

FCL to AL
Englewood, Fall 1918

Thursday night Aunt Lucy and Uncle Jack came up, and Aunt Lucy did some automatic writing and got messages that purported to be from Uncle Hammond, Grandmother Lamont, etc. It was very interesting and your brother Corliss was much thrilled by it[1].

---

[1]TWL's only sister, Lucy, was married to John Palmer (Uncle Jack) Gavit and fancied herself a spiritualist in touch with the Great Beyond and dead relatives.

TWL to AL
New York City, October 1918

On Friday I went to Washington at the President's request and had an interesting interview with him. I wanted him to know that the Evg. Post stood with him on the principles of a just peace for all the belligerents and would support him to that end. He is afraid that we may grow so martial as to become revengeful, which would be unfortunate . . .

FCL to AL
New York City, October 1918

Darling Austey,
What do you think of Wilson's answer to the German peace offer? I thought it very good and terribly clever. It is going to force Germany to state her exact position. Senator Lodge[1] makes me sick. I wish someone would blow him up. I think his criticism of Wilson is disgusting.

FCL to AL
Englewood, November 1918

Tommy is up in Boston for Sunday to say goodbye to all his best girls. He starts Wednesday morning for Camp Zachary Taylor. I cannot bear to think of it. He will be inducted into the army sometime on Wednesday, and then I shall have absolutely no control over my boy any more. Even if he is dying, I cannot go to him unless his commanding officer lets me. How I hate everything military—with my whole heart! How I hope Wilson will be able to bring about his just & healing peace so we shall not sow any seed for future wars.

[1]Henry Cabot Lodge, Republican Chairman of the Senate Foreign Relations Committee, was already lobbying against ratification of the Treaty of Versailles with its League of Nations covenant.

FCL to AL
Englewood, Fall 1918

Darling old love,

The epidemic[1] is very bad here. The hospital is full, and they are opening the Field Club as a sort of annex to it. There are many families where the father, mother and children are all down with it, and there is no one to nurse them or cook for them. I am just starting off to wash dishes in the Influenza-Pneumonia hospital at the Field Club. I don't want to go a bit, and I'm scared—but no one knows it. I wouldn't have anyone know it for anything. I'm going because I think I ought to. I am so glad you are in Pomfret . . .

In 1919 TWL participated in the Paris Peace Conference as a member of the American Mission. He was representing the U.S. Treasury Department as one of the nation's leading financiers.

TWL to FCL and children
Hotel de Crillon, Paris, April 15, 1919

The dinner last night was quite interesting. I had a nice three-cornered talk with Orlando and Papa Joffre[2]. They did most of the talking, almost all of which I understood, and I made a few intelligent ejaculations in French. I asked him (ed. Orlando) what, in his opinion, had been the cause of the war. He asked me whether I recalled the reports of certain medical scientists who described the habits of a perverted lot of persons who would actually reach down, pick up a handful of soil and eat it. "Well," said

[1]The worldwide flu epidemic reached its peak that October when 40,000 deaths in the U.S. alone were recorded.

[2]The dinner was hosted by Colonel House, senior member of the American Mission, and included Premier Orlando of Italy and Gen. Joseph Joffre, France's field marshal and hero of the battle of the Marne.

he, "that reminds me of this hunger for earth that seemed to have possessed so many peoples and to have been their undoing." I talked with Mr. Paderewski[1] and then with his wife who was wringing her hands and deploring the fact he would never play the piano again . . .

FCL to AL
Englewood, Fall 1919

Last Monday Mr. Hoover dined with us. I like him and do hope he will be our next President. We talked about all sorts of things, a lot about labor and strikes. When he left, I said, "I hope you do not think I'm a Red, Mr. Hoover. You know I am going to work for you for President." He said, "Mrs. Lamont, if ever I am President, my first act will be to jail you for a Bolshevik!"[2]

FCL to AL
Englewood, October 1919

Friday night we went to a small select dinner to meet the King & Queen of the Belgians. I didn't know until two minutes before the King & Queen came in that I had to curtsy to them. I fell into a panic because I couldn't remember whether you put your right leg or your left leg back to make a proper curtsy. But I did it by intuition when the King stood before me. I was perfectly willing to curtsy to the King & Queen. They have been brave and noble people. But when it came to the little Prince, the American eagle perched on my shoulder and screamed. I thought, Why should a woman of my age bob to this little boy? And I wouldn't. And I was the only one who didn't. I suppose I was very silly and provincial.

---

[1]Jan Paderewski, the renowned pianist and newly named Prime Minister of Poland, whose wife feared that statecraft would end his music career.

[2]Herbert Hoover, then U.S. food administrator, would be elected President in 1928.

FCL to AL
Englewood, Fall 1919

I had luncheon with John Drinkwater[1] and his wife. He is the man who wrote *Abraham Lincoln* which has been the great success of the London stage for almost a year. Tomorrow I am going in to New York to have luncheon with Hugh Walpole[2].

FCL's and TWL's interest in writers was no accident, though they preferred to gravitate toward the English, rather than the American, literary scene. TWL had been president of the Harvard Crimson, the undergraduate daily, and had begun his career as a financial reporter for the old New York Tribune. His brother Hammond had taught English at Harvard and Brown Universities before becoming editor of the Evening Post and, later, The Nation, a weekly magazine well regarded in literary circles. TWL's cousin Gordon Lamont was the Post's city editor for a time. His brother-in-law Jack Gavit had been the Washington bureau chief of the Associated Press and written several books. FCL's sister-in-law Anne Parrish was a prize-winning novelist noted for her satirical works. Although, as a boy, TWL had devoured novels from Dickens to Verne, he found it harder to pursue leisure reading as his business career took off—a turn that moved FCL to observe, in a letter to CL, "It is strange to me that he never wants to read, but I suppose his wonderful energy is what makes him such a power."

That energy and power drew TWL and FCL into elevated social and artistic circles. It also made them indefatigable world travelers. TWL's repute as the Morgan empire's unofficial secretary of state granted him and FCL the kind of receptions abroad usually reserved for visiting potentates. Ever since their first trip to London near the end of the last cen-

[1]John Drinkwater, English poet and playwright.
[2]Hugh Walpole, prolific English novelist and social historian.

tury, England had been their favored port of call. But their list of destinations expanded rapidly. In some countries they reveled in the headiest of official welcomes. Mostly, it seemed, they had to contend with queasy ocean crossings, dysfunctional roads and hostelries, mysterious foreign germs, harebrained fellow tourists and ungrateful locals. Their meals ran the gamut from cold mutton to eels and seaweed soup.

FCL to AL
Imperial Hotel, Tokyo, March 11, 1920

Occasionally I find myself at dinner between two men, neither of whom speak a word of English, and then there's nothing to do but eat. The eating always takes about three hours. Very elaborate, perhaps fifteen courses.

The other night I sat next to a man who spoke English well and with whom I was able to discuss everything—politics, the position of women, etc. He told me that Japanese ladies always smoke pipes instead of cigarettes. I said I should love to learn to smoke a pipe, it would be such fun to shock my husband. The little Jap nearly rolled out of his chair with glee, and said, "Madam, allow me to send you a pipe." The next day the most beautiful pipe arrived, in gold and lacquer, along with a lovely silk tobacco pouch. That evening at the hotel, when all the others took their cigarettes out after dinner, I took my pipe out and smoked it.

There's been an auction going on for the last two days. The Russian Ambassador has been selling off his various works of art and I've had a frightful time trying to prevent Father from coming home laden with the most awful junk you can imagine. I go with him to the auction every morning and sit close beside him and beg him, with tears in my eyes, not to buy some huge cracked umbrella stand. I haven't been very successful and we are coming home with barrels of third-class stuff.

Last night we went to the theatre. The play was not especially interesting. I slept soundly through one entire act. But I came on strong at the end for the wedding ceremony which seemed to consist of a loud clapping of hands by the onlookers on stage. Another night we

AL growing up

went to a third-class theatre, where we sat on the floor and tea was brought in for the audience in funny little boxes covered in quilted tea cozies. The man sitting next to us was suffering from cold feet, for he took off his stockings and put his bare feet in the tea cozy to keep them warm. It was a delightful performance, with two women committing hara-kiri on stage in the presence of their husbands who sat calm and unmoved while the wretched women groaned in their death agony, rolling about on the floor in the most frightful way. The audience seemed to take this quite as a matter of course.

TWL to EAL
Astor House Hotel, Shanghai, March 30, 1920

Well, here we are in China at last, where all the women wear trousers and the men skirts. It is too queer to see all these fat Chinese ladies waddling along in pants and the young girls Austin's age carrying their hands in their trouser pockets. The men's skirts trail in the rain & wet and are a terrible nuisance. Your mother thinks it's wonderful to have the fashions reversed this way.

We left Japan on a French steamer which was very comfortable except that we had nothing to eat and nothing but wine to drink, and all the machinery and plumbing were constantly out of order. Last night, as we approached the coast of China, a deep fog came up and your mother was sure another steamer would run into us. But we landed this morning all right and have already been about the town. Lots of people were here waiting to see me. The Chinamen are more than human. If they think there is a chance of Santa Claus turning up, they are all waiting close by at the bottom of the chimney.

Among those waiting for TWL was a group of students who were persuaded that the international bankers were seeking to enslave China. They wished to make their point by stoning TWL when he emerged from his hotel. Forewarned, TWL invited the students up to his suite for tea and spread a little balm. The stoning was postponed.

FCL to Lucy Gavit
Astor House Hotel, Shanghai, April 1, 1920

I don't like China. The want and hunger and suffering stare one in the face every minute. You tell the doorman to whistle for a ricksha, and three men come running up, thin, hungry, eager, and you have to make a choice. The man you choose is usually physically unfit—perhaps a swollen, infected ankle—and you know that *you* ought to be dragging *him,* not vice versa. But if he doesn't drag you, he will starve to death. So there you are. It makes me very unhappy.

FCL to AL
Peking, April 20, 1920

In most places shopping is a vulgar pastime. But here it is an art, a sort of glorified apotheosis of shopping. You go down a dirty, narrow little street and enter a villainous dark doorway, and all of a sudden the passage turns, and there you are in a sunny court with gay flowers in pots and lovely stone carving. That's it! It's the element of surprise in everything that makes the life here so wonderful and stimulating. You never know what's going to happen next. You expect to see an automobile, and a camel arrives. The thing that arrives is always beautiful or terrible; it's never commonplace.

FCL was introduced to the English tutor of the young Emperor, perhaps the most knowledgeable westerner on Chinese civilization and religion she had ever met. And one Sunday she visited the Summer Palace of the late Empress Dowager. Her guide, a Mrs. White, had been Lady in Waiting to the old Empress.

FCL to AL
Peking, April 20, 1920

. . . It was wonderful to go through the Palace with her. We would look into the different rooms and she would tell us just where the Empress used to sit, what the young Emperor used to do. Sometimes she would end up by saying, "In this very room I have seen with my own eyes the Empress Dowager have a eunuch beaten to death or a servant condemned to death." It made your blood run cold.

We came across the lake in a boat with six Chinamen in the back, rowing in their queer fashion, and a tall eunuch who used to be the boatman for the Empress Dowager in the days of her greatest glory. He recognized Mrs. White and told her that he was now getting $3.70 a month. He was very poorly dressed. Mrs. White said that when she had seen him before, he had been most gorgeously arrayed in bright-colored embroidered coats and had had lots of money.

I couldn't help feeling that the spirit of the old Empress Dowager was haunting every place and looking with great disapproval on this foreign invasion.

Later that year, the Middle Kingdom a fading memory, the TWLs partied with royals of another kingdom as the New York social whirl continued.

FCL to AL
New York City, November 1920

Last Tuesday was the grand Davison dinner for the Prince of Wales. I am glad Harry and Kate love these big affairs. I should have died if I'd been in their shoes. There were about 750 people at the dinner, all sitting around at small tables in the big Waldorf ballroom. Then the orchestra played a slow march, and a procession of notables—Elihu Root[1], General Pershing[2], Ambassador Grey[3], etc.—walked slowly down the aisle between the tables. Then, in the distance, you saw their Royal Majesties slowly proceeding, "King Harry", "Queen Kate", and the P. of W. walking between them. Gosh, I'd have hated to have walked down that aisle as they did, but I guess I am queer.

Everybody who was anybody in New York was there, all dressed up fit to kill. I had a brand new pink and silver brocade in which I looked hideous. Elihu Root made an awful speech, boring and full of platitudes. The little Prince made an awfully good one. It won all hearts. He seemed about Cor's age and used "splendid" all the time in his speech—New York's skyscrapers were so "splendid", he was having a "splendid" time, etc. He seemed like such a nice little boy . . .

The next night was the big ball at Mrs. Whitelaw Reid's[4]. It was in a private house, of course, and a much smarter affair. Father was in Cleveland and I went with Uncle Charles[5]. It was the most elaborate party I've ever attended. The little Prince danced like mad. He never went near the fine supper in the dining room. He danced with all the fluttering "debs", made love to all the pretty ones, and was very dignified and Prince-like with all the plain ones. I had a few minutes' talk with him.

If only the rest of her family had taken religion as seriously as she did, FCL might have eased off on her evangelizing. TWL had a definitely more relaxed attitude.

---

[1]Elihu Root, former Secretary of State; winner of the Nobel peace prize.

[2]Gen. John "Blackjack" Pershing, commander of the American Expeditionary Force in Europe in World War I.

[3]Sir Edward Grey, ambassador to U.S.; Britain's Foreign Secretary in World War I.

[4]Elizabeth Whitelaw Reid, a leading benefactor of humanitarian causes and wife of the editor of the New York *Tribune.*

[5]Charles Corliss, FCL's older brother and a successful businessman.

FCL to AL
Englewood, November 1920

I persuaded Eleanor and Father to go to church Thanksgiving Day, telling them it was to be a short service of song and prayer with only a few minutes' sermon. Instead, we had a strange man who preached forty minutes of the worst talk I have ever heard. Father and Eleanor behaved awfully. They played tic-tac-toe and giggled, and so did Mimi[1].

Other challenges confronted FCL as the Twenties roared in. She roared back with gusto, flailing errant politicians, the hired help, obstreperous, sub-performing kinder. It was the golden age of Ruth, Dempsey, Capone, Lindbergh and Man O' War. The headlines and radio news told of the Scopes trial, the Red Scare, the elections of Harding and Coolidge. The country was awash in speakeasies and flagpole sitters. It had turned from the sacrifices of war to the giddy self-indulgences of the new decade, from the idealism of the war years to the "enjoyment of tremendous trivia", in Frederick Lewis Allen's phrase.

The Lamonts focused their Presbyterian rectitude on other things, like Wilson's losing struggle to persuade America to join the League of Nations, and their expanding family. Their fourth child, EAL, was now ten; their oldest, TSL, was graduating from Harvard and would soon marry. TWL, nearing the peak of his power, was the Morgan partner who, in the words of one later historian, most typified the Jazz Age—a "small miracle of sophistication" who added an urbane 1920s' gloss to his bank's image. In between advising Presidents and making global loans, he danced the Charleston and sought to imitate Bobby Jones on the fairways. FCL attended to domestic matters, protecting her cubs from the evils of bathtub gin, tobacco, racy books, and false religions.

[1] Julia Parmelee "Mimi" Corliss, aged 77, FCL's mother.

Sky Farm, circa 1919
(Courtesy of North Haven Historical Society)

The country may have been caught up in a love affair with Henry Ford's newfangled motorcar, but FCL found it just another challenge to her inventiveness. In a letter to CL, years later, she recalled driving back from Crater Lake in Oregon when the gas tank had sprung a leak. "I set all you children to chewing gum frantically (having hitherto blackly frowned on you for doing it), and the gum patched the hole and lasted until we reached home."

The Lamonts had also just settled into their new summer home on the island of North Haven in Maine. They christened the property Sky Farm.

FCL to AL
Englewood, January 1921

Corliss was down for Sunday. He arrived Friday evening and I took him to hear Sir Philip Gibbs[1] lecture on Ireland. The Sinn Feiners[2] have been hostile to P.G. every time he has lectured. From the start of the lecture, the gallery was hostile. There were hisses, hootings, catcalls. Of course, Corliss wouldn't stay with me, but went up to the gallery where he had the time of his young life. Every time the gallery hissed England, Corliss clapped his two big hands very loudly, so that they all threatened to break his head.

[1]Philip Gibbs, English editor, war correspondent and novelist.
[2]Sinn Fein, the Irish nationalist movement and political wing of the Irish Republican Army.

One lady was so noisy that Corliss remarked to a policeman (the gallery was packed with them, all Irish) he thought the lady should be put out so others, who had paid good money for their seats, might hear the lecture. The policeman answered, "Stop insulting that young lady. She has as much right here as you!" "Yes," said argumentative Corliss, his mother's own child, "but you are not doing your duty to permit this noisy riot." "Ha" said the policeman, "You criticizing the New York Police Force, you fresh young cub?" "I sure am," said C. At that, three other policemen gathered, and the Irish girl pointed at Corliss and said, "That's the fella that insulted me," and with more passion than logic she added, "What did you do in the war? You look like one of them English slackers. My brother died in France!"

Well, they told Corliss they would arrest him if he didn't leave the gallery immediately, and Corliss, feeling every inch a hero, said to go ahead and arrest him! They didn't, thank goodness. A nice time I should have had hunting all over and finally bailing him out of a police station at 3 A.M.

FCL to AL
New York City, February 1921

Saturday we lunched at the White House. Everyone said that W.W. would not come down to the dining room, as he never had done so at any social gatherings since his illness[1]. But he did and I was delighted. After luncheon Mrs. W. took me all through the White House, upstairs and down, then the President sent for me and I went and sat beside him and had a nice long talk. I longed to tell him that he was making a terrible mistake to keep Debs[2] in prison, but he looked rather frail and I thought perhaps I had better not . . .

Sunday we went to the Belgian Embassy for luncheon. I sat next to a man in uniform. Of course, I hate anything military and I have

[1]Woodrow Wilson had been incapacitated since his stroke in late 1919. The crisis had left his wife Edith in virtual charge at the White House during the last weeks before the newly elected Republican President, Warren harding, moved in.

[2]Eugene Debs, the Socialist leader, had been jailed for violating the Espionage Act of 1918.

never taken the trouble to learn what all their silly little stripes and buttons and stars mean, so I didn't know whether I was sitting next to a general or a private. But wishing to make conversation, I said, "I am going to preside at a disarmament meeting next week, can't you give me some ideas on the subject?" He turned on me in a fury. "Madam, it's talk like yours that is dangerous for this country!" "But," I said, "I haven't talked any yet. Anyway there's no use your getting so furious with me, because you look exactly like my friend Henry Nevinson[1], so I can't help adoring you." He calmed down a little then, but proceeded to give me a tirade against disarmament. He turned out to be General March[2], the chief of staff of the American army, higher even than Pershing!

TWL to TSL
New York City, March 16, 1921

I had an interesting day in Washington last week. I saw President Harding at the White House, and asked him if he wouldn't make a fresh appeal for Chinese famine relief along the lines of a statement that I submitted. He was very much interested in the suggestion, promised to do it, and was as good as his word.

FCL to AL
New York City, Spring 1921

Aunt Lucy & Uncle Jack are spending a great deal of time with the spooks now, about four nights a week. One spook told them that if only they perservered, they could see Joe's spiritual body in the room with them. That isn't my idea of spirit. I don't believe we can ever "see" it with our earthly eyes. But who knows?[3]

---

[1]Henry Nevinson, English newspaper correspondent and essayist.
[2]Gen. Peyton Conway March, Chief of Staff, U.S. Army
[3]Joseph Lamont Gavit, Jack's and Lucy's only surviving son, had died of typhoid fever the year before at the age of 21.

FCL to AL
Englewood, Spring 1921

Wednesday night we dined with the Roosevelts. I sat next to Franklin D.[1] I thought he was rather dull, and he seemed to have rather a poor opinion of women. I mean, I am used to having men talk to me about interesting affairs as if I were a man, too—and he didn't.

Mademoiselle Gringoire[2] is awfully nice—but she snores! I don't know what to do! I am wretched! Isn't there anybody in the world who doesn't snore? I am going to advertise: "Wanted—A non-snoring Governess. Not particular as to morals & mind. High Salary."

TWL to AL
S.S. Adriatic, April 13, 1921

I didn't want to come over here a bit. I like springtime in America. I was away in China all last spring, and in Paris the spring before that. So I hated to come . . .

Your mother has written you of the people on board. John Galsworthy[3], the novelist who writes very modern stuff, is in real life as proper and solemn as an owl. He wears a monocle. Your mother has long curly conversations with him about Love and the Universe. But I don't get on very well. They are all very human in that they enjoy and consume prodigious quantities of our special food which was sent to us by kind partners—fresh asparagus and such. They lap up our cream and drink two bottles of burgundy each night on me! Then John Drinkwater will read us some of his latest verses in a singsong voice that puts me to sleep in no time . . .

We are due at Southampton Friday. Our only excitement was to run into a burning ship at sea in the night, and send a small boat to the rescue. I'll ask Eleanor to send you my illustrated account of the

---

[1]Franklin D. Roosevelt, then Assistant Secretary to the Navy, would be elected President in 1932.

[2]Mademoiselle Gringoire, a newly hired household staffer.

[3]John Galsworthy, author of *The Forsyte Saga* trilogy and other works.

adventure. Take care of yourself and don't let Corliss get engaged while we are gone.

That fall TWL and FCL visited Mexico where TWL had been asked by the local government to help resolve its debt problems. TSL had graduated from Harvard the past June and was off to England for a year of postgraduate study at Cambridge University.

FCL to AL
New York City, September 1921

Yesterday we went to see Tommy off, Eleanor, Father and I. The *Olympic* was as crowded as in June—Mary Pickford[1] had my old rooms and was quite the Queen. All the crowd was there . . . It was bedlam. I am never going to see anyone off again.

FCL to TSL
Englewood, September 29, 1921

I went to luncheon with Herbert Croly[2] to talk over Mexico and the affairs of the world. We went to an Italian restaurant in Greenwich Village, and it was so full of fleas that they walked and hopped all over the dining room table. I was simply fascinated with trying to kill them before they hopped—it was real sport—and I could hardly listen to the words of wisdom that fell from Herbert's lips. I got all mixed up and thought he was talking about Mexico when he was really talking about Japan, and made the most frightfully inapropos remarks. But I caught the flea . . .

---

[1]Mary Pickford, the film star and wife of Douglas Fairbanks.
[2]Herbert Croly, editor of *The New Republic.*

The lunch with Croly proved to be a fine training exercise for the challenge of Mexican hotels.

FCL to CL and AL
San Antonio, Texas, October 1921

Here we are, just starting off again for Mexico. Spent the night at a hotel here to get a little rest. The heat has been *too* terrible.

The more I hear about Mexico, the worse it sounds. The latest is scorpions. One bite and you're a goner. They drop on you from the ceiling. Also, small-pox, heaps of it. It flies in at your window. And, of course, typhus-bearing fleas over everything!

FCL to TSL
Mexico City, October 1921

Do you know how I feel? I feel "stung"! Mexico City has been painted and written up as if it were the City of God, the New Jerusalem and Paris all rolled into one. What it is is a dirty, fifth-rated continental town. How under the sun I am going to spend two solid weeks here is beyond me.

The train trip down . . . horrible road beds, bad engines. We jolted and bumped and stopped and wheezed and backed all night long every night for five nights. When we reached the border at Laredo several men got on the train to see Father, and we gathered them up at every station as we approached Mexico City. Each one wanted to tell Father how to run his mission, just what to say to Obregon[1], and just how to put Mexico on her feet financially.

We are staying at the house of an Englishman named Holloway, why I do not know. He is the president of the Vera Cruz Railroad and the house is situated at the junction of three trolley lines, so you know how happy I must be. Father's secretary and his interpreter are

[1] Alvaro Obregon, president of Mexico.

staying at a hotel which is full of bedbugs and fleas, so I try not to mind the trolley tracks. The first night we were here a large rat jumped on Father as he lay in bed and nearly scared the wits out of him. He came bursting into my room about 2 a.m., saying he didn't know whether it was a rat or a large Mexican snake[1].

FCL to TSL
Mexico, October 1921

I am feeling much happier because I have moved out to a little village about 10 miles from the city, where there's a wonderful old inn kept by a French woman. It is very quiet here and I can sleep finally. Also, I've bought a mosquito net which adds to my happiness. I spent my first night here killing huge tropical spiders and red ants an inch long . . . The road coming out from the city to the inn used to be infested with bandits a short time ago. So when I go out to dinner and come home late, I have an extra man in the front seat of the car, armed with a gun. It's quite exciting!

In addition to dining with President Obregon, whom she described as a "red-faced brigand", FCL spent time with some of the grandees of the old aristocracy who had prospered during the rule of the dictatorial Porfirio Diaz, deposed a decade earlier.

. . . They are really charming people, well-bred, and oh, how they hate the present government! Of course, they have lost everything in the Revolution, even their furs & dresses & jewels. The generals occupied their houses and stole everything. When these people go to the opera now, and look around at the government people in the audience, they can identify their own diamond ornaments on these

[1]TWL seemed to attract rodents. Years before, while a student at Exeter, he had been bitten one night by a rat in his dormitory room.

other women, mistresses of the various generals, etc. It's really amusing to go from tea with the Grand Senora Algara to dinner with Obregon. The aristos all want me to tell Father how dreadful the present government is, so I find myself very popular.

At the last minute TWL changed his departure schedule and left Mexico City two days earlier on his private car attached to a San Antonio-bound train. In San Antonio, FCL and TWL learned that the train they were supposed to have taken had been waylaid and wrecked by bandits who confessed they'd planned to kidnap TWL and ransom him for half a million gold pesos. FCL was relieved to return to New York and move into the Lamonts' new home on Manhattan's upper east side.

FCL to TSL
Englewood, December 28, 1921

Uncle Jack & Aunt Lucy came to Christmas dinner. They had just come from Joe's grave and so were all broken up.

When I die, Tommy dear, do not visit my grave Christmas day. I shall not be in it, but somewhere round the Christmas tree, or where the fun is—that's where you'll find me. I think, too, I shall try to come back to Sky Farm because I love it so. I shall never spend my days in a cemetery . . .

TWL to TSL
New York City, January 6, 1922

In one of your recent letters you express great doubt as to the value of this year abroad.

What I had in mind when I urged you to go to Cambridge was not simply the work that you would do at Cambridge (which I hope will turn out not inconsiderable), but the fresh ideas and fresh outlook upon affairs that you will gain from the many different people

TSL on bicycle trip in France, 1921

you will meet and the scenes that you will visit. It has always been important for a man to start his active business life with as broad a point of view as possible. But now it seems to me it is of much more importance with the world in the state that it's in.

Perhaps you won't realize this when you first start in work. You may wonder how it helps you—licking stamps or writing figures in a ledger or running around on errands for people—to have spent a year in England. But as the days and years roll by, I think the realization of it will come to you, and I hope it will come in enabling you to take a saner and a more tolerant view of people and things than otherwise you might have taken. If you gain such a point of view, certainly you can handle men and affairs more wisely and be more of a factor in your world.

I only know that as I look back over the last twenty-five years of my "misspent" life, I would have given at least five years of it to have had the chance you are having this very moment.

TWL to TSL
New York City, February 7, 1922

. . . Uncle Jack is pretty much obsessed with this medium business. They have had a couple of people there lately who summoned poor Joe's ghost so plainly that they could all see it, dressed in his sailor suit that he had when he was a member of the Harvard Naval Unit. A very nice poem came along from him the other day—'over the wire', so to speak.

Not that TWL and FCL totally dismissed the medium business. TWL insisted to TSL that he took no stock in it, "except certainly there is something, somewhere, that we don't by any chance understand." FCL, after attending a seance, thought there was "something real about it all, a real force of some kind which we poor humans know practically nothing about." If neither of them took it truly seriously, FCL was still known to swear by a Mrs. Ottarson who had apparently cornered the market for curing colds without medical or pharmaceutical assistance. "I have had only one cold in two years," FCL wrote AL. "Mrs. Ottarson seems to have cured them for good."

TWL to AL
Grove Park Inn, Asheville, North Carolina, March 1922

Last summer I missed with you kids completely, and I should love a little expedition together. We shall all be together for August and half of September anyway. But at North Haven I am beset with daily telegrams and telephones from the office. That's why I welcome a few weeks far enough away to be rid of them.

Your mother says she has written you about Tommy and Ellie Miner. Well, she is a fine girl and intelligent and ought to make Tommy happy. It came sooner than I expected. But then I was in love with your mother while I was still in college. But I was so utterly lacking in worldly goods that I didn't dare try to sign her up, and the delay gave us more time to be sure—which was probably a very good thing. Tommy isn't so handicapped, lucky lad.

FCL to AL and CL
Paris, May 1922

I have been leading what might be called "the lower life"—thinking of nothing but clothes and frivolity and food. Father is dancing his way through Paris, and I dance, too, when I am not too dead with fatigue.

One day last week I went down in the country to see my one-legged Frenchman, Geoffrey[1], his wife and eight children. It is really the happiest home and happiest children I know anywhere, and they are as poor as church mice. Geoffrey is doing a wonderful monument, a war memorial, for the little village of Valusondois. We went to see

[1]Possibly the son of Jean Geoffrey, a French genre painter who lived from 1853 to 1924.

it in the pouring rain. It is a fine thing and I wish to goodness I was some sort of an artist. I believe they are far & away the happiest people on earth. Mrs. Geoffrey is wonderful, too. She is the most selfless person. She simply radiates life and happiness as I believe only the very unselfish can do . . .

TWL to EAL
Hyde Park Hotel, London, May 5, 1922

In Paris last Tuesday I had a long talk with Poincaré[1], the Premier of France. He was a short, little old man, very precise, very intelligent, and very clear in his language although he spoke only French. I told him that I feared France was not very popular in America just now, and that I thought it would be well for him to say some things that would serve to counteract some of the wrong impressions that France had created. He told me he wanted very much to do that and asked whether I thought the speech he would make at Verdun on June 1st, in accepting the memorial medal to be presented by the United States to the City of Verdun, would not be a good occasion. I said, yes. Then he asked me if I would not write out for him what I would say if I were in his place. I said that, with much reserve, I would try and submit something.

The next day the American Ambassador wanted me to tell him what Poincaré had said. When I told him, he replied: "Well, I've just been working on *my* speech presenting the medal. I want you to let me send it to you so you can revise it and make it fit in with what you suggest to Poincaré that he say." I think it is all quite a joke.

FCL to CL and AL
Hyde Park Hotel, London, May 1922

I caught an awful cold in Paris, which I brought to England and which has cramped my style considerably on this lovely island. It was hard luck to have the reddest of noses to greet all my poets with whom I have been very gay (when I haven't been half-sick in bed).

---

[1]Raymond Poincaré, Prime Minister of France.

The first Sunday here we went to the Masefields.[1] Tuesday we dined with Neville Lytton[2], Wednesday with the St. John Ervines[3] and went to see John Galsworthy's play "Loyalties". Thursday Mr. and Mrs. Galsworthy took us to see "Loyalties" again and we had to pretend that we had never seen it before.

Saturday we motored down to Cambridge to see Tommy. I was disappointed that Tommy seemed so lacking in affection for Cambridge. It seemed so wonderful to me. He had undoubtedly been homesick. As for me, my heart leaps out at the beauty of Cambridge and Oxford. I feel that in some previous life I must have lived in one of those old ivy-hung courtyards and drunk long and deeply from the Book of Knowledge. Too bad none of it stuck to me, but I have such a feeling of kinship with the place it's uncanny.

FCL to AL
Sky Farm, Maine, July 5, 1922

Last evening I went over to the Choates[4]. All the children were setting off fireworks on the dock. Of course, I went to the dock with Eleanor. It was pouring rain, but it didn't seem to make any difference to the fireworks. You never saw such wild confusion. There were about 20 small boys and girls. Mr. Codman, Mr. Story and I were the only grownups. Sandy Choate was on the rampage. He was lighting everything within sight, regardless who was near or far. The other little boys were just as bad. The first thing I knew, a huge rocket went whizzing by my head, nearly killed Mr. Codman, and went zig-zagging through the crowd.

After last evening, a night in the trenches with a few German shells overhead would be mere child's play. At least one would know what direction the enemy was.

---

[1]John and Constance Masefield. He was by then England's renowned saltwater poet and playwright.

[2]Neville Lytton, a leading English landscape painter.

[3]St. John Greer Ervine, Irish playright and novelist.

[4]The Choate clan's patriarch was Joseph H. Choate, onetime U.S. Ambassador to Britain and a distinguished lawyer in the late 1800s.

There were occasional exceptions to the quality of parental advice FCL and TWL offered.

FCL to CL
New York City, September 13, 1922

I spent Monday evening with Col. Thompson[1] at his house in Yonkers and listened to a very interesting discussion carried on by a Mr. Dula, the president of the Liggett-Myers Tobacco Company, as to the advantages of chewing tobacco. Mr. Dula claims that chewing tobacco is the most healthful occupation in the world, making this assertion with a good deal of reasoning and force. He was brought up in a town in Missouri where everybody chewed tobacco, and it had the lowest death rate of any town in the state. He recalls one family of eight sons and two daughters, all of whom were taught to chew tobacco at the age of three. They all grew up to be six feet tall and large in proportion. It seemed to me that he proved his case beyond question (ed. All the Lamont sons smoked.)

TWL and FCL had been just a year breaking in their new Manhattan home on East 70th Street, a grand four-story townhouse in the Tudor-Jacobean style with mullioned windows. Among their earlier receptions was a luncheon for the wives of TWL's banking colleagues from around the country.

[1]Probably William Boyce Thompson who had played an influential role in urging recognition of the new Soviet government and in 1919 had founded an institute for plant research in Yonkers, New York.

TWL's New York City townhouse at 107 East 70th Street, ca. 1921 (Wurts/Museum of the City of New York)

FCL to AL
New York City, Fall 1922

It was Main Street let loose. They didn't attempt to talk much, but sat and stared for two solid hours. They stared at me, my hat, my dress, the room, the furniture, the rugs, etc. The time set for the luncheon was one o'clock, but they began coming at five minutes after twelve. When I came down at 12:45 the room was full. But they were rather a nice lot of women, mostly from the South, Texas and West Virginia . . .

FCL to CL
New York City, Fall 1922

I was so interested in your letter—"the ravings of one who does not know where he is at," you say. Well, why *should* you know where you are at at this time? (ed. Physically, he was still at Harvard.) Everything opens out to you so wonderfully, everything is so exciting and stimulating—infinite possibility, all potentiality. It is too soon for a many-sided person like you to begin eliminating potentialities. Why don't you go on as you are for awhile, being thankful that this most amazing & wonderful world can stimulate you and woo you in so many different ways? Do not try to narrow them down just yet.

There are many disadvantages in being a rich man's son, but there is one advantage. Do take it. You haven't got to decide to settle and earn your own living immediately. You are given time—which is a really precious gift. Go on with all your many interests and some day one will emerge. You can't force it, or you may get the wrong one.

I think what you say about the greatest need of the world today being a new religion or a revitalized old one is absolutely true. The life of the spirit goes on and on, but it needs restatement from time to time. For whatever God meant man to be or to do, the whole universe assures us that he did not mean him to stand still.

What a queer person he must have been who was surprised when you said that for you the greatest pleasure was real hard work. I thought that was more or less accepted, at least if the work is creative in any sense, and most good work is. I have never been able to decide myself which is the most lovely thing, the joy of creating something or the joy of a sort of communion & deep contact with the minds of people you love. Perhaps they are corollaries. I don't know.

Goodbye, you old nice darling thing . . .

Some creative work never got FCL's seal of approval.

FCL to CL
New York City, Fall 1922

The more I think about "Rain"[1], the less I like it. The longer I live, the more convinced I am that it is a terrible mistake to let the imagination dwell on sin and ugliness. A thing as well done as "Rain" makes a very vivid picture—a picture utterly sordid & terrible—with no special significance, nothing leading out from it, no suggestion. "Whatsoever things are pure, whatsoever things are lovely, whatsoever things are just, whatsoever things are of good report, think on these things". That's good advice for body & soul.

FCL to CL
New York City, November 1922

I have come across two Bible verses that I think are really corking. One is, "Not by might, not by power, but by my spirit, saith the Lord." Goodness, how that hits me. I try so hard to do this and do that, and all the time the thing to do is to be still and let God do it through you, use you, just let yourself be a channel for a bigger force. Take more time for thought and less for action. I pass this on to you because I am not sure but what you need it, too. The other verse is, "Be ye transformed by the renewing of your minds." I could preach a wonderful one on that . . .

FCL, however, could no more forsake the hyperactive life, doing this and doing that, than TWL could take monastic vows. Her commitments in-

[1] *Rain,* the play based on Somerset Maugham's tale of illicit love, had been a smash hit on Broadway that season.

cluded the Foreign Policy Association, birth control, the starving children of Central Europe, the women's Trade Union League of New York, the Academy of American Poets, The Journal of Philosophy, various Shakespeare and poetry reading societies, as well as support of those leading women's colleges that comprised the so-called Seven Sisters. A typical letter to one of her children began: "I have had a very busy week with lots of committee meetings where it takes all my self-control not to throw the fire tongs at the woman opposite me." FCL was also the consummate soft touch for needy acquaintances.

FCL to CL
New York City, November 1922

I have dozens of lame ducks just longing for me to get home—a single man without any engagements; an actress out of a job; a reader of Gilbert Murray's plays[1], a very nice woman, eagerly looking for engagements; an artist and his wife (English) who want orders for portraits; and another singer, an English woman . . . What am I going to do for them all?

FCL had a typically ad hominem view of politics, domestic and foreign.

FCL to AL
New York City, November 1922

Old Clemenceau[2] has arrived and, Lor' sakes, what a fuss everyone is making over him. A horrid old man, say I. I suppose he is more responsible than any other one man for the Versailles Treaty and the present state of Europe. He is cruel and vindictive. And yet New York

[1]Gilbert Murray, the British classical scholar, playwright, and Regius Professor of Greek at Oxford.

[2]Georges Clemenceau, France's wartime Premier, whom TWL had gotten to know during the Versailles Treaty negotiations.

is making such a time over him. Even Father is giving him a reception. I am glad it is for men only and that I shan't have to see the old wretch and tell him how wonderful he is.

TWL to CL
New York City, November 21, 1922

You may have seen by the papers that I gave a reception yesterday at the house for old Mr. Clemenceau. There were about seventy-five there, including Elihu Root and others. I introduced Chauncey Depew[1], aged 87, to Clemenceau who is only 81, and Clemenceau put his hands on Depew's shoulders and said, "Why, I am a mere babe!" Then he turned and asked me how old I was. I admitted to being a little over fifty, whereupon he said, "I shouldn't think they would dare let you go out without a nurse!"

TWL to CL
New York City, November 1, 1922

To my mind there is a curious connection between clear thinking and clear writing. The man who learns to write clearly learns to think clearly. This may sound like putting the cart before the horse. It is true that the man who has got something clearly in mind usually has the capacity to write clearly. Yet it is not always so, and the point is that when a man finds himself compelled to put his thoughts down on paper, and to express them clearly and forcibly, he sets to work to think much more clearly than he has ever been compelled to do before. Please think it over before you dismiss this idea of some work on the *Crimson.*

---

[1]Chauncey Depew, formerly president of the New York Central Railroad and U.S. Senator from New York.

FCL was less taken with the virtues of journalism, undergraduate or otherwise.

FCL to AL
New York City, January 1923

That clipping from the Ladies Home Journal filled us all with intense rage. Tommy asked Father in awful tones if he would permit him to write a letter to the Editor. It was a nasty article.

Did I write you of the announcement of Tommy's wedding, which appears in three New York papers, including the Post?[1] That also filled the family with intense rage. It said Tommy and Ellie had been married last May (ed. They would be married that coming April.) It sounded quite discreditable. Father made the *Post* and *Herald* print huge retractions in large type.

By early 1923, TSL was back from Cambridge and starting his career at the Morgan bank. CL was a junior at Harvard, Austin a senior at Exeter and bound for Harvard in the fall. Only EAL was still at home.

FCL to AL
New York City, January 1923

I went to the Cosmopolitan Club to hear Coué[2]. It was most interesting. But best of all, I was admitted to his clinic Saturday morning. We all sat around in a big room and he went from person to person, asking what was the matter. I sat between two awfully queer men. When Coué came to my left-hand neighbor, he asked what was

[1]The New York *Evening Post* had been sold by TWL a year earlier.
[2]Émile Coué of France, student and exponent of hypnotism and auto-suggestion; introduced system of psychotherapy known as Couéism.

TSL and his fiancée
Elinor Miner on North Haven, 1922

the matter and the man almost yelled, "Nerves, nerves!" Another man, when asked, said modestly, "Imperfect elimination." "Ah," said Coué, "You mean constipation!" and the poor man looked awfully uncomfortable. Then he cured several of various pains and that was intensely interesting. I am going to another clinic tomorrow.

FCL to AL
New York City, February 25, 1923

Many, many happy returns of the day!

I hope every good thing will come to you this coming year, and that you will make it count for a good deal. You have everything worth having—health, wealth, a good mind, a fine character, a loving mother and father and brothers and sister. All good things are yours. So much has been given you, you are under a special obligation to give back to the world all you can . . . What is this I hear about your staying out all night in an auto, bitterly cold weather, and no warm clothes on? Write me all about it *at once.* You needn't think, Austey Lamont, that just because you are 18 you can keep things from your old Ma. I won't have it.

TWL to CL
New York City, March 26, 1923

Ten thousand congratulations on your twenty-first! Long life, prosperity and happiness attend you! Bless you. Keep young and brave and true.

When I was 21, it was just after the opening of my senior year at Harvard, September 30, 1891. I roomed in old Thayer Hall on the third floor, #16, looking out on Appleton Chapel. One afternoon I was writing in my room—a special Sunday article for the Boston *Herald* which paid me the then princely salary of $50 per month. A gentle tap came on the door and I murmured, "Come in." Nothing happened but another and louder tap. Then I yelled, "Come in, you old fool!" In stalked President Eliot[1] . . .

[1] Charles William Eliot, president of Harvard (1869-1909).

I can remember those days vividly and yet they are really long ago. If, on the day I was 21, I had looked forward to thirty years, I would have said that the end of that period would have meant life was almost over. Yet now that that time has gone, life seems more full than ever of interest & even excitement. There are more problems than ever waiting to be solved; there are more real things to be done. Every day the world is a more vital place to live in. Every day offers more chances to help along. Much of my life for two years past has been devoted to helping poor Mexico to her feet, to improving relations between Mexico and America. The accomplishment of that task is one of my daily prayers.

Well, isn't this the darndest birthday letter—three lines about you and the rest about myself! Your mother is better for her neuritis but still not perfect. Lord Cecil[1] arrives tomorrow.

FCL to Mimi
Englewood, April 9, 1923

Dearest Mother:

Well, our great week is over! Lord Robert left Friday morning. He is a most remarkable man, one of the few really great men in public life. He has that rare quality that comes from throwing oneself, one's ambitions, life, everything, into a big cause. You can't imagine what last week was like. Lord Robert's secretary, Mr. Baker, stayed at the house. His other secretary, Mrs. Strachey, was there all day and took most of her meals. Two typists were also there banging away on typewriters all day. The telephone rang every minute, the doorbell rang every minute. But it was all in the best cause in the world, the League of Nations. No more war for my boys!

---

[1] Viscount Edgar Algernon Robert Cecil, Member of Parliament and Cabinet minister, had collaborated with President Wilson in drafting the League of Nations Covenant in 1919. FCL, a Presbyterian like Wilson, shared the same liberal pieties and belief in the League as he did.

That spring, following TSL's wedding to Elinor Miner of Rochester, New York, TWL and FCL sailed for Europe on a business-and-pleasure trip.

TWL to AL
S.S. Olympic, May 2, 1923

Despite the presence of his Lordship (ed. Cecil again) it has been a dull voyage. No burning ships at sea, no rescues. After lunch we adjourn to the Ritz Palm Garden and talk—silly most of the time, sensible sometimes. Lord Robert has a scunner against H.G. Wells[1]—thinks he has no elements of creativeness or original thought, but simply a clear manner of phrasing "to tickle the ears of the groundlings" (he calls it), i.e., us poor mortals who live down close by the earth, with never a head in the stars.

TWL to CL
S.S. Olympic, May 3, 1923

Your mother and I have been driven to employ fiction. I wrote up an account of the breaking in two of the *Olympic* in mid-ocean in a terrible hurricane, my narrative being dated on a raft at longitude 33° & latitude 45°. Your mother wrote vividly of the theft and recovery of her pearls. It was so probable that I fear Eleanor will really mourn their loss . . . In Paris I expect to meet the members of the Austrian loan commission. Then I hope to start forthwith for Italy to get a line on Mussolini and his new way of ruling[2].

---

[1]H.G. Wells, the novelist and historian, had by then written *The War of the Worlds* and his *Outline of History* and was fast becoming a regular at FCL's and TWL's New York home.

[2]Benito Mussolini had introduced fascism to Italy as his new way of ruling.

TWL to EAL
Hotel Excelsior, Rome, May 15, 1923

Now I could write you an essay on the home life of the ancient Romans. I am quite mad about Rome. I had never been here. Your mother had, ages ago, when a young Italian followed her & knelt on the steps of St. Peter's, clasped his hands and proposed to her.

TWL to CL
Rome, May 16, 1923

This trip is as bad as the Mexican one when your Mother, one Sunday morning, ran away to a bullfight and left me to go on an expedition to see the oldest cathedral in Mexico. This time it was at Monte Carlo.

Last Sunday, just as the church bells were ringing, we were ushered into the famous Casino, and there, although it's past the season and was only 10:30 in the morning, were half a dozen huge tables filled with players—*Rouge et Noir, Vingt et un* and other games of chance. About one-third of them were women, not a single pretty one in the whole outfit. Most of the people looked sad and dispirited. I was hoping for an E. Phillips Oppenheim[1] denouement: some ravishing creature suddenly to give a scream, then attempt to thrust a grain of cyanide of potassium in her mouth; then I was to rush forward, clutch her wrist in an iron grasp, and say, "Foolish & misguided woman, do not cast away the life that God has given you. Live to cherish that flower of beauty that is yours. Do not despair. Here is a note for a thousand lira. Take it, invest it wisely, and live happily hereafter!"

N.B. The lira is now worth five cents.

[1]E. Phillips Oppenheim, author of novels of adventure and intrigue.

TWL to AL
Rome, May 18, 1923

Yesterday we attended a lunch at the American Ambassador's in the Orsini Palace which they are lucky enough to rent. There was one Duchess and two Countesses there, but these titles are common as figs in Italy. Your mother spends most of her time in bed to get fit and in training for the intensive campaign in Great Britain. I have done considerable sight-seeing. Yesterday afternoon I attended an outdoor performance of *Oedipus Tyrannus* by your old friend Sophocles. The King attended and had the honor of occupying a seat very close to me, where he could get an excellent view of me. I also could see him very plainly, a short little man dressed in a field marshal's uniform, not at all impressive. But they say he is much loved.

FCL and TWL regularly urged on their children greater moral sensibilities. TWL believed that moral sense was far more important than intellect, and liked to quote the French philosopher Henri Bergson's saying that "one of the qualities of the intellect is its inability to understand life." On the eve of AL's transfer from Exeter to Harvard, he issued a firm parental warning.

TWL to AL
New York City, September 26, 1923

Only one thing bothers me and that is the question of your smoking. When I was in school and college . . . it was not simply a question of expense with me, because I could have scrimped and worked out a package of cigarettes every day or two. It was other considerations which I think apply equally to you. Health is one of them. Every doctor with whom I have ever talked tells me a boy is much better off without smoking until he has reached maturity.

There is no question about this. The next consideration is that of habit. When you start smoking at your age, it grows on you steadily & insidiously until it is fastened hard. So please just lay off the thing for a while.

Newly married TSL and wife were setting up house—too nonchalantly for FCL's taste.

FCL to AL
New York City, Fall 1923

Getting Tommy & Ellie into their new house is a hard job. They take it very casually. Last night they both came out and shut the door, leaving the keys inside. There was no way to get in, and the gas man, the electrician, etc., were all scheduled for this morning. But they didn't worry. We got a locksmith to open the door, at some high price, but the gas man came and couldn't get in. They are very amusing but utterly irresponsible. I can't imagine what they would do if they didn't have us.

TWL to CL
Englewood, October 21, 1923

I am more glad than I can say that you spent a weekend with Aunt Lucy & Uncle Jack. It is hard to put oneself in their shoes. But if I were ever inclined to be critical of them, I have only to think how rudderless I should be if all my children were swept off at one blow; if all that I had built upon for twenty years fell to pieces like a house of cards; if the tenderest cords of my feelings were suddenly torn apart and seemed as if they would never heal again. All of that, and more, is what that gentlest of souls, Aunt Lucy, has gone through, and Uncle Jack no less.

CL in his early twenties on a camping trip

FCL's romantic musings, which occasionally bordered on the occult, often contained descriptive historical nuggets.

FCL to TSL
Boca Grande, Florida, February 1924

The water here is a marvelous blue-green, sometimes turquoise, the sand a saffron colour. The palms grow down to the water, so you can sit on the beach yet be in the shade. It's just like those islands of romance where lovers get wrecked. The men play golf every morning and fish almost every afternoon. It really seems all wrong to play golf here, all out of place. One ought to tie up one's head in a red bandanna and dig for pirate gold.

This really was a haunt of pirates and there's $30,000,000 in gold buried in these islands somewhere. Yes, sirrie, there is, honestly. Gasparilla flew the black flag on these waters about 1800. He was a gay pirate and loved the ladies (ed. long before the word "gay" was misappropriated). He used to raid the Mexican coast and carry off lovely Spanish ladies. He kept twelve at a time. Whenever he captured another beautiful damsel, the least attractive of the twelve had to make way for her, and was taken out & promptly beheaded. That must have been some inducement to keep your hair waved and your figure trim!

FCL to CL
New York City, March 1924

I think just about the hardest thing in life is to know how far to compromise, how far to do evil that good may come, to what extent the end justifies the means. I am all mixed up in it in my own life.

I can't bear it when someone says, "(President) Coolidge had to take such and such a position, for you must remember, Florence, he is dealing with imperfect human beings, etc." One can't help feeling that a big, strong personality of buoyant faith could do the big, strong thing and sweep imperfect human nature along with it, making the humans better than they knew they were, making them respond to big ideals. Oh, it could be done, I am sure.

Perhaps men do not do it because too much emphasis is put on accomplishment—I myself rather believe in triumphant failures.

FCL's thoughts were driven by reports of CL's protest at Harvard over the issue of free speech, specifically whether Harvard ought to deny a podium on its campus for Eugene Debs, the labor leader and perennial Socialist candidate for President. "I agree with you," she said in the same letter, "that a great university can get along without the money of an alumnus who thinks it wrong to hear Debs. I also think college boys ought to hear pacifism and socialism discussed." FCL would have been less enthused about granting Senator Lodge a podium to discuss his views on the League of Nations or the poet Byron to offer his views on monogamy.

Your essay on Byron is awfully interesting. I must confess I know Byron very little. I never had the desire to go further. It isn't a bit because he was not faithful to his wife or any other woman that I don't like him, but because he was so innately vulgar & petty & jealous and lacking in dignity of soul. He had none of the big sins. A man can only express what he is. An artist who isn't much of anything in himself can't express anything very big. He may be most sinful, according to our moral standards, but there must be something big in his nature. I do not find in Byron anything that suddenly reveals beauty or wisdom or truth to me—that enlarges my intimacy with life. Byron does not change me at all.

TWL to AL
New York City, March 22, 1924

Professor Gulick spoke in very complimentary terms of your work in Greek. I told him I thought you came naturally to your genius in

Greek by reason of the fact that your grandfather—my father—was for some years a professor of Greek before entering the ministry. During all my boyhood and youth at home I never failed to see my father once or twice a day reading the Greek Testament. He read the text from a little volume which I still have and which, as a matter of fact, was picked up by a Union soldier in a rebel rifle pit after the Battle of Culpepper Court House in the Civil War. I imagine that some rebel school teacher or minister had turned soldier, was killed in the rifle pit, and the book fell from his pocket . . .

TWL to AL
Englewood, June 8, 1924

All I want to say is that all through life you will find that candor is a great asset, that concealment is a great liability. It is like a canker in the nose, it eats into your heart and gives you a feeling of heaviness and oppression. To those with whom you have relations your candor is the great and open hallmark of character. Everyone should be able to say of you for all time: "We know where he stands. He has nothing to conceal. He says just what he means."

The wreckage of war increasingly occupied TWL's professional and public life. Restructuring the world's economy in the wake of World War I became the purview of the leading bankers, TWL in their forefront. He traveled incessantly, negotiated tirelessly. The League of Nations proposal had become a hot domestic political issue and FCL hit the lecture circuit on its behalf. Inevitably, the Lamonts moved in ever higher social and cultural circles. TWL threaded his way with soft-spoken charm and politesse. FCL found it all both exciting and excessive. In discourse she preferred confrontation to diplomacy, the straight-forward thrust rather than the subtle parry. Sooner or later, she and TWL would have an epistolary falling-out over politics and politicians as a genre.

TWL in 1920s

In the summer of 1924, with the Presidential election campaign warming up, they were off to Europe. TWL went as a key advisor on the Dawes Plan to settle the question of Germany's reparation payments to the Allies.

FCL to TSL
S.S. Celtic, July 4, 1924

We are having an awfully nice time, very gay for the children, all sorts of games and races. Corliss won the pillow fight. Tonight there is a fancy dress ball. Father presided at the Ship's Concert last night and did very well. The concert itself was the most awful thing ever. It would be impossible to imagine anything so bad.

FCL to TSL
4, Audley Square, London, July 1924

Father is having the time of his young life!

Prime Ministers wait on his word and send for him at all hours. The house is filled with Ambassadors, Ministers of Finance, Belgian, French, Italian. I don't know who is enjoying it more, Metcalfe[1] or Father. I say, "Metcalfe, is Mr. Lamont ready for luncheon?" "Ready for luncheon! Why, Madam, he is in conference in the morning room with Premier Herriot[2], the American Ambassador is waiting for him in the back drawing room, in the front drawing room the Italian Finance Minister has been waiting for an hour to speak to him, and President Norman[3] of the Bank of England is just coming up to the door in his car."

What we should have done without a house, I can't imagine. I shudder to think what life would have been for me and the children with one sitting room at the Hyde Park Hotel. We should have had an ambassador hidden under each bed and a finance minister in every closet!

[1]George Metcalfe, the Lamonts' imperturbable English butler and longtime chief of staff of their household.

[2]Edouard Herriot, Premier of France.

[3]Montagu Collet Norman, Governor of the Bank of England.

FCL to TSL
Geneva, August 1924

Well, Paris is over. It was cold and rainy. Father was just about as busy as in London. The telephone rang every instant. Cablegrams, telegrams, letters arrived in masses, with little boys in uniforms waiting for answers. Two or three secretaries were always on hand in the sitting room. Father dictated letters while he dressed. Our last dinner, Austin obligingly sat, holding the telephone to his ear with one hand while he tried to eat his dinner with the other, for Father was trying to get Mr. Mellon[1]—and you know what a French telephone is. All was excitement.

FCL seemed at times more forgiving of Germany than the demanding bankers and statesmen. "I have never met a German, an individual, that I did not like," she wrote one of her children. "Yet we speak of the nation as if they were all hell hounds." CL by this time had graduated from Harvard and was taking a postgraduate year of study at Oxford. TSL, meanwhile, was back in the heat of New York, missing all the flurry in London and Paris, feeling a bit sorry for himself and his tedious daily grind at the bank.

TWL to TSL
Geneva, August 22, 1924

I just got your blue letter about the office. I wrote Arthur Anderson[2] today and asked him to put you in the Bond Department before any German loan came off—if one ever does. I can realize how you feel about the office work. It is no doubt terribly routine and irksome. I never had to go through it. But I had to go through what to me seems much worse: grinding anxiety, with a feeling of living in

[1] Andrew W. Mellon, Secretary of the Treasury.
[2] Arthur Anderson, one of the younger Morgan partners.

a house of cards likely to tumble down on my head at any moment—and that at the very time when your own arrival in this world was expected hourly.

You are learning to know men. I have always had a feeling (though I know nothing about it) that our office was not well organized, having grown up from a little family affair into a really huge bank, without any real change of antiquated systems or personnel. The time will come when change will have to be made. Then your experience will be of the greatest benefit.

TWL had been instructed to remain in Europe through September and early October to help negotiate the Allied powers' loan to Germany as part of the reparations solution. He shuttled between Paris and London where FCL had settled in as a guest of the Masefields in Oxfordshire. On October 1, a first son was born to the TSLs and a cable reached FCL at the Masefields. By chance, the Irish poet and dramatist William Butler Yeats was visiting the Masefields the afternoon the cable from New York arrived. He looked at FCL in some amazement and said, "Do I hear that you're a grandmother?" She nodded. Yeats paused. "Not thus did grandmothers appear when I was young," he said. The new grandson would be christened Thomas W. Lamont II.

FCL to CL
New York City, October 1924

Thank you for your fine letters. I am sorry your room is bare. I don't think the Huxleys[1] would mind a bit if you added a comfortable chair or two, and a table, and, above all, reading lamps. Father and I both feel you should have plenty of lamps and good ones.

[1]Julian Huxley, the eminent English biologist and writer, and his wife were frequent visitors of the Lamonts in New York. CL, at Oxford, was temporarily living with them off-campus.

FCL in early 1920s

Nothing is so precious as your eyes, except your immortal soul, and I am not sure even of that. Do make yourself comfortable—never mind the money. You are always too economical. When I see the way money is wasted in this family . . . How I wish I could run over and make your room attractive.

Corliss, I am in disgrace, deep disgrace. I really get so red-hot passionately indignant over the Republican campaign and that little timid 3rd-rater, Coolidge, and the lies they tell about the League of Nations[1], that I disgrace myself every time I go out to dinner or luncheon. I wish I did not feel so passionately about things. But perhaps this is what gives life so much colour to me.

Sunday I met the B——s at the Pomeroys. You know I can't bear either of them, and I just couldn't keep my mouth shut when they said things. I answered back. And soon I found myself in the most awful controversy with lisping, cooing J who has the brains of a canary. To argue with her is like hitting a pillow. You can't dent it, it comes right up smooth again. Everyone in the room stopped talking and formed a ring around us to listen, as they do in prize fights. J kept saying there were dreadful things in the League that America couldn't subscribe to. I said, "What? Name one." She said, "Oh, I can't." I said, "Just one, tell me only one." She said, "There isn't time." I said, "Loads of time. I can stay a whole hour longer!" (Loud applause). J gets very red and mad, etc.

I am speaking alot for the League. I made a good hit at Spuyten Duyvil. I am speaking in Englewood on the 7th and the 10th, and in New York for the League of Women Voters on the 25th. Do buy some warm winter underclothes.

FCL to AL
New York City, November 1924

I had such fun on Election Day. I went to the polling place, wearing a large and conspicuous Davis button[2]. (I don't think there was another Democrat in our section except the Howeses). I would find myself standing next to some dyed-in-the-wool Republican like Stuart Lyman, and I would say unctuously, "Good morning, Stuart. What

---

[1]Critics of the League argued it was at best a utopian concept premised on an idealized world purged of such human failings as conflict, greed, hubris and faith in the balance of power among nations. Wilson's 'open covenants' diplomacy was said to be unrealistic.

[2]John W. Davis, the Democratic nominee opposing President Coolidge.

a beautiful day! I hope you are voting the straight Democratic ticket, as I am!" Then I'd watch with delight the angry red creeping from his neck to his face, while he sputtered, "I'm voting the straight Republican ticket, as you should be." "Why should I?" said I, and then we'd have a glorious set-to. It was a wonder I wasn't arrested and put out of the place. It was such fun. I stayed half an hour, just prancing around showing my button. I love being in the minority, championing a lost cause.

In the event, FCL's favorite lost in a landslide to Coolidge whom TWL had backed. FCL's disappointment, coupled with CL's early soundings about a future political career, elicited this letter from TWL a few days after the election.

TWL to CL
New York City, November 6, 1924

Taking up first a minor point, I do not consider that you will find yourself handicapped because your father is a member of the firm of J.P. Morgan & Co. Any connection with this firm I consider just as much an asset as a liability, and I consider that this applies to politics . . . I think if you were to take a vote among people who know anything about the matter, they would applaud the efforts we have been making to help reconstruct the world, and so better to establish conditions of peace.

As for being in politics in America, I don't feel at all as your mother says she does as a result of the recent presidential election. She seems to feel that in a country that voted by such an overwhelming vote to make Coolidge president it is utterly hopeless to go into politics. I think exactly the contrary. If I were going into politics, I should want to go into them in America. And I should consider that the result of the election last Tuesday was a spur to go in and help things rather than to stay out.

TWL to AL
New York City, November 13, 1924

After one of your mother's talks in Englewood a woman came up to her and said that if the League of Nations was the fine thing she described, why had it not stopped the Great War in 1914? You can see the benefit we are getting from having given women the vote.

In the last weeks of 1924, the social pace quickened. Homebound Eleanor (EAL) had become a precocious 14-year-old. That Christmas, Lord and Lady Cecil again descended on the Lamonts. Cecil, whom TWL had first met at the Paris Peace Conference, was a leading proponent of the League. According to a prominent American observer, Bernard Baruch, he "epitomized the best of British aristocracy."

FCL to CL
New York City, December 1924

I gave a big tea for many of the workers in the Foreign Policy Association. I tried to keep it as small as I could to make it a little more intimate. James G. called up and said could they bring a friend. I said certainly. They arrived, a whole phalanx of weird people, half a regiment, marching up the steps, six of them at least. I became hysterical as one freak after another made his and her bow. Then, at the very height of the tea, the queerest figure of a woman appeared. She had on queer high-button boots, a loud plaid black-and-white coat, and a queer hat with a heavy veil over it. Everybody stopped drinking tea and looked shocked. I think they thought she was a Bolshevist. I knew she had not been invited and was wondering what to do, when Father came up and took her in tow and introduced her to Lord Cecil. I could hear her talking in queer tones to him, and then it finally dawned on me—it was Eleanor.

An exhausted FCL collapsed on her bed, having entertained the Cecils nonstop before finally bidding them farewell. TWL escorted the Cecils downtown to their steamer on the morning of their departure for England. They barely made it.

FCL to CL
New York City, January 1925

We were having a real blizzard. They left the house in loads of time, two cars, the maid and bags following. It took them over an hour to get to 21st Street (the boat was sailing from 14th Street) and then they got in the most awful traffic jam. It was eighteen minutes to ten at the time, and the boat sailed at ten. Father saw it was impossible and jumped out into a snow drift. His Lordship did the same, Her Ladyship did the same, the fat maid did the same. Then Father saw three black men on the sidewalk, and by paying a king's ransom got them to carry the thousand bags. Lord C rushed ahead. Father, with a heavy bag on one arm and Lady C on the other, ploughed through the drifts. The three black men showed a tendency to disappear down the side streets with the baggage. They had to be rounded up at every corner. The fat maid would not hurry. Neither prayers nor oaths moved her. But they finally reached the steamer at six minutes before ten—a real triumph for Pa.

The Cecils were among the more notable adornments in TWL's and FCL's lifelong Anglophilia. Cecil's father, Lord Salisbury, had been Prime Minister to Queen Victoria in the late 1800s. Victoria herself had been observed by TWL and his new bride when they visited London in 1896 on their first trip abroad. TWL recalled how each afternoon in the park near their hotel the aging Queen would appear in an open landau drawn by two horses. TWL remembered the tiny sunshade she always carried, her "puffy little eyes, her pendulous cheeks, her rather grim look, and her figure which was not wrought with grace." Twenty years later, the Lamonts had befriended the poet John Masefield who had come to New York to promote the Allied cause in World War I, and they had begun a long association with other English literary lights.

CL, meanwhile, was thinking of declaring a boycott of all extracurricular activities at Oxford and confining himself to his books. TWL, perhaps recalling Montaigne's stricture about making the fullest use of life, thought this a retrograde notion.

TWL to CL
New York City, January 9, 1925

It's a fact that you can go ahead working on your books from now till you are ninety. The opportunity, however, for meeting and discussing matters with charming and intelligent English people at your impressionable age comes only once in a lifetime. It will not recur. You would do well to take advantage of it. You will find that by the end of the year you will have accumulated a sort of background of ideas that will be of value to you all the rest of your life.

I consider one of the chief weaknesses of our public men today is that they are in entire ignorance of what the rest of the world outside America is thinking. They would be much more sympathetic, much more helpful, if they could put themselves in the shoes of men across the water for just a little while. It isn't necessary for them to adopt that point of view, but it *is* necessary for them to get it.

FCL to CL
New York City, January 16, 1925

Helen Blake had a dinner consisting of me, Manley Hudson[1] and the Ernest Hockings[2]. Manley and Agnes left to attend some meet-

[1]Manley Hudson, Harvard professor of international law and prominent American jurist.
[2]William Ernest Hocking, noted philosopher and Harvard professor.

ing and Helen and Ernest and I sat around the fire. We talked philosophy and pseudo-religion as hard as we could for two hours. The trouble with Jack G's[1] philosophy is that he always mixes up matter and spirit. But they belong to two different realms of Being. Spirit uses matter, is the flowering out of matter, but must never be confused with matter. Thought & extension are fundamentally different.

FCL was wearying of the lecture circuit.

FCL to CL
New York City, January 1925

I have just come back from the wilds of New Jersey where I went to speak on the L. of N. I sat in a crowded room and listened to a fat and high soprano sing, "Butterfly, butterfly, where are you going?" While the sleet beat against the window panes, I thought, "Oh, where am I going and why am I in this awful place?" But it's all over now and I am safely home again. I go to Boston in a day or two to speak for the League. I am awfully sick of speaking.

FCL to CL in Oxford
New York City, February 1925

What fun to meet John Buchan[2]. Did you read his *Three Hostages*? I wonder if he really believes in hypnotism to such an extent. Ask him. You say nothing about the Murrays[3]. I am much disappointed that you are not seeing Gilberto more intimately. He is one of the rarest and most beautiful souls on earth, with a lovely sense of humor. Wasn't it thrillingly interesting about his telepathic experiences? . . .

[1]Uncle John Gavit.
[2]John Buchan, the Scottish author, a.k.a. Lord Tweedsmuir.
[3]Prof. Gilbert Murray and his wife Mary.

FCL to TSL, AL and EAL
Hotel Excelsior, Rome, April 12, 1925

Early in the morning we started for Capri to see the Brett Youngs[1]. We went up a perpendicular railway to the little piazza of Capri. It was exactly like the drop scene of some Italian opera—blackbearded, villainous-looking men stalking about with red kerchiefs around their necks; a great clock tower and an old church opposite; on the farther side of the piazza, a precipice some thousand feet high with the sea far below, blue and brilliant. We motored around the side of the mountain to Anacapri where the Youngs live, a little villa situated in the midst of a growth of lovely gray-green olive trees. I asked Brett Young if *Cold Harbor* had any existence in fact or was just an imaginative story, and he said every word of it was true, which made cold shivers run down my back . . .

Here in Rome, Father rushed off to meet the King. I can't imagine why anyone would want to meet this little puppet of a king, but Father thought he ought to on account of the Italy-America Society. Corliss and I came later and had a merry time on the train (ed. From Naples to Rome). Corliss insisted on buying a huge bottle of dreadful wine at a small wayside station, and drank it hilariously without any cup all the way to Rome . . .

This is Easter Sunday and I wonder what you are all doing. I hope you are out in Englewood and that you had the big hare on the table as usual, and lots of Easter eggs and an Easter hunt. The thing I enjoyed most here was going to a Good Friday service at St. Peter's. We went about half-past six just as it was growing dark. The church in the dim light seemed incredibly large and mysterious. The music, sung by choir boys unaccompanied by organ, echoed and re-echoed through the great building. As we turned to go, the music stopped and there was the most frightening rumbling sound followed by a terrific thunder. I thought at first it was an earthquake and couldn't understand how the thunder and rain could have come on us so suddenly out of the serene blue sky. But it was only part of the Good

[1]Francis Brett Young, the English novelist.

Friday ritual, meant to represent the rending of the temple in twain and the storm that took place at the moment of Christ's death. To the people there it was the most holy moment of all . . .

Sunday we motored to Florence to stay with the Berensons[1]. I think it is the most perfect house I have ever been in anywhere. It is on a slope behind Fiesole, with a most enchanting view of the mountains. Their garden is one of the most beautiful spots in the world. Everything in the house was absolute perfection, almost too perfect for ordinary mortals. It made me feel as if our house in New York was a sort of barracks.

Mr. Berenson, of course, is recognized as the best art critic in the world. He is about ten years older than Father and full to the brim of the most interesting ideas, although he is perhaps a trifle too precious, too exquisite. When I went for walks with him I felt like a great strapping peasant woman in both body and mind. Every day he would make out a sort of little program of the things he thought most worthwhile my seeing in Florence, and would talk to me about them and explain just why they appealed to him so. I feel as if I had had a regular debauch of ideas and beauty . . . and now I feel intensely dull and all ready for the low-browism of Paris.

Nothing, of course, stirred FCL like England in the spring. On her own, TWL having sailed for home, she visited CL at Oxford, joined the Masefields in producing one of their homemade theatricals, and immersed herself in the local literati.

FCL to TWL, EAL, TSL and AL
Hyde Park Hotel, London, April 1925

Dearest Tom, Darling Eleanor, Nice Tommy, Beloved Austin,

[1]Bernard Berenson, the art critic, and his wife presided over I Tatti, their home and a mecca for European and American intellectuals.

The weekend at Oxford was wonderful! I arrived amidst all the excitement of the play[1]. I sewed up the sleeves of Judas, I helped John add gilt ornaments to Pilate's footstool. I arranged the chairs and draped the seats for the chorus. It was grand fun.

At the play I sat next to Bernard Shaw[2]. He is certainly the very most amusing person on earth, even more so than H.G. (ed. Wells). Sunday afternoon Corliss and I motored to the John Buchans for tea . . . Tuesday the Huxleys gave a luncheon for me . . . H.A.L. Fisher[3], the Warden of New College, took me all over his wonderful 14th-century house, from garret to cellar . . . Tuesday afternoon we went to tea with Corliss' tutor, a great philosopher with the looks of a merry gnome. I had sat up late every night cramming up on his philosophical lectures, and I hope I made a hit. My poor brain hasn't worked so hard in years!

I found it restful to get back to London where I could have a bath and all the blankets I wanted. I was so cold in Oxford that I slept in woolen underclothes and woolen stockings and a sweater. Lunched with Gilbert Murray who was in splendid form, then rushed home to an early tea with Walter of the Sea[4]. Then I spent an hour with a crazy man and had another tea. This is the man Nevi asked me to help. Do you remember, Tom? Well, he is just about the most interesting person I have ever met. But entirely crazy. How I do love mentally unbalanced people. I always get along so beautifully with them.

FCL to CL
New York City, Fall 1925

Your remarks about insanity are very naive. Of *course,* everyone with a good imagination commits all sorts of crimes mentally. I have

---

[1] The play in all likelihood was *The Trial of Jesus,* first published by Masefield in 1925 and privately performed in the music room at Boars Hill, the Masefield home, on May 9th that year. FCL and others may have attended a dress rehearsal.

[2] George Bernard Shaw, the playwright, critic and wit.

[3] Herbert Albert Laurens Fisher, historian who helped reorganize the system of public education in England.

[4] Walter de la Mare, the poet.

shot Senator Lodge with a pistol, carried in my little black bag, many times. I have committed every sin you can think of. I think almost everyone has, except the most unimaginative people who never daydream. The only difference between us and lunatics is that we control it, our thoughts, and they do not. As for your persecution complex, I think it comes from your innate modesty . . .

FCL to CL
New York City, October 1925

Mrs. D played the violin divinely. I envied her It must be wonderful to do one thing supremely well, to have complete mastery over some form of self-expression. I am sure that is about the best that life has to offer, except to walk with God—that would be a mastery, too.

Machinery was what eluded TWL's mastery, anything above the level of pencil sharpeners and typewriters.

FCL to AL
Englewood, Fall 1925

I have just come back from the village with Pa. He tried to turn around in the middle of the street and stalled his car—tried seven times to back it, and stalled it seven times. In the meantime, hosts of autos, enroute for the ferry, were blocked. All got furious and when he stalled it the seventh time they all hooted and shouted, and a policeman came. I do think Pa risks his life every time he drives an auto.

TWL was baffled as well by his youngest son's attraction to certain fields of science. As he wrote AL at one point: "About oceanography and that sort of thing, I don't seem to be very deeply impressed with the great im-

AL in his early twenties

portance of it in the development of the world at large. Probably that is because I am ignorant. I really don't know what it means. If, however, you do go into science, I hope it will be some line that is of wide importance. Perhaps oceanography is big enough for you. I should doubt it." (A quarter of a century later, AL had become a prominent anesthesiologist and FCL had deeded one of her and TWL's country estates to Columbia University to be a major oceanographic institute.)

FCL to CL
New York City, Fall 1925

Here is a letter from Mimi that I want very much to have you read. It's just one point of view about philosophy, that it is often unsettling and sometimes paralyzes one for other work. Of course, it needn't. I regard it somewhat as a disease. If you have it, you have to work it out. Happy are those people who do not have to go clean down to the bottom and foundations of things, who can go on singing at their work without bothering as to whether the foundations of the universe are of steel or sand. Well, I am not one of them. I never could rest day or night, literally, until I found some reason for believing that the foundations were laid in justice, in love, in beauty. Also, I would always infinitely rather meditate with someone on space or causality than I would to make an apple pie.

FCL to AL
New York City, Fall 1925

I am very busy over clothes. I hate buying dresses more than any other form of activity. I am exhausted by it. I was never meant to be a woman. I am worried to death over the League.

FCL to AL
New York City, November 1925

I am *dee-lighted* that you carried a L. of N. banner and got jeered at. Bully for you!

FCL to AL
Asheville, N.C., November 1925

Lady Colefax[1] is coming to visit me on the 14th. We are going to have great goings on. Gosh, how I dread it! I no sooner get rid of the Drinkwaters than Lady C arrives. What is going to become of my reading and my meditations and my inner life?

FCL to AL
New York City, December 1925

I have just had a nightmare of a meeting at my house. The Non-Partisan Association asked me to have a World Court meeting and serve tea afterwards. They said about 70 people would come. So we prepared for 80 and got some chairs from the cateress. But when 4 o'clock came, a perfect horde descended on the house. They came up & up the stairs until there were 235 of them. We brought down every chair from the bedrooms, bathrooms, kitchen, every chair in the house, and still there were crowds of people standing, sitting on the floor, etc. They all seemed to be old ladies over seventy, with crutches and canes and bad legs. Then the tea! We sent out for more cups and saucers, and Metcalfe made 650 sandwiches, and we had thousands of little cakes. In five minutes there wasn't a sandwich left or a cake. They seemed to be not only crippled but starving. Thank heaven, it's over.

FCL to AL
New York City, January 11, 1926

I am leading a horribly busy life, so filled with good works that it's revolting—teas for the League of Nations, a luncheon here at the house to raise money for the Women's Trade Union League, another big luncheon for thirty women who are at the house, too, and I have got to make them a speech that will "inspire" them. But none of these

[1] Sibyl Colefax, doyenne of London's literary-social set.

things is anything compared to this awful debate that I have undertaken for the Colony Club. All the Colony Club women are taking it very seriously. The other day I went to a meeting where it was being discussed, and I said, "What I am going to say doesn't worry me nearly as much as what I am going to wear," and they all looked perfectly solemn and said: "You are quite wrong, what you are going to say is much more important." My opponents are Miss Rachel Crothers who writes and produces plays and is quite a woman, and Mrs. Charles Tiffany who is extremely clever. My partner is Miss Ruth Morgan. I have made myself the most awful bore at every dinner and every luncheon I have been to, asking at each one for a definition of leisure, for this is the subject of the debate. The debate runs this way: Resolved, that the women as represented by your club membership have too much leisure. We have the negative which I think is much the best side.

TWL took time to share thoughts and reminiscences with his two youngest children. (AL was marking his 21st birthday at Harvard; EAL had just started at Milton Academy.) As always, he was the quintessence of tact.

TWL to EAL
New York City, March 17, 1926

A nice letter from Miss Goodwin[1] says some very complimentary things about you. It pleases us very much, and if only your report, which I am returning to the authorities, could speak a little more strongly about your ability to concentrate, we should feel there was nothing lacking.

---

[1]EAL's housemother at Milton.

EAL, North Haven, 1922

TWL to AL
New York City, February 25, 1926

What was I doing on *my* 21st birthday? I had just become a junior at Harvard because it was September 30th, 1891. I had spent part of my summer holiday on Mackinac Island far up the trails between Lake Superior and Lake Huron (ed. actually between Lake Michigan and Lake Huron). We had taken a cruise up to the Snow Islands on a leaky sailboat. We had dug up the skeleton of an Indian and done other crazy things. I returned home and went out to Englewood for the *first* time to see your mother. Mimi and Grandpa[1] were very cor-

[1]Wilbur Fisk Corliss, FCL's father.

dial, but they looked upon me as nothing but one of the crowd of boys who came and went, fascinated by your mother's charms.

How swiftly the years have run since then! Then, my own mother of blessed memory was only 49, much younger than I am today. To you, thirty years hence, looking back, it will seem but a few fleeting hours. I hope & pray that in these coming years you will be able to look back, as I am able to, over a happy life and upon children who have yielded every satisfaction and delight because they have been strong and true, and because (in Josiah Rogers' phrase) they have already begun to have "the wisdom to comprehend and the courage to endure the business of life."

The Lamonts' spring passage to Europe included stops in London, Paris and Spain where TWL met with King Alfonso in Madrid and with FCL visited Granada and Seville. Their bon-voyage gifts led to a fine snafu.

FCL to TSL and wife Ellie
H.M.S. Mauretania, April 1926

I am having such a hard time thanking people for the right things. Father and Metcalfe opened all the packages while I was taking a nap, and got all the cards mixed up. I have just written a letter to Mitchell Follansbee thanking him for a large Virginia ham, and Father came in and said, "He didn't send you a ham, he sent you tulips." But I refused to write it over. Life is too short, and anyway I have thanked him for *something*. Mrs. Morrow sent the ham, but I have already thanked her for a barrel of clams. William Porter sent the clams, but I have thanked him for his "beautiful flowers." I hope he thinks that's a poetic way of describing clams . . .

We sit at the Captain's table, which is a bore as they all eat like rhinoceroses. One man has nine courses every meal. It takes him 1½ hours, and we have to sit and watch him. You have to stay until the

Captain leaves, and he waits for the human pig. Well, I'm not perfect myself, and Father doesn't seem to mind the people.

FCL to CL
Hotel Ritz, Paris, May 1926

In Seville, Father had a strangely infected nose, all swollen and dreadful. After several days of pain he cabled Mrs. O (ed. the same Mrs. Ottarson who had personally cornered the health-cure market), with the result that the nose from that minute on started to get well. It is too queer for words. The day the Masefields left I caught the grippe, and Mrs. O was not so successful with that. But moderately so. In fact, I felt so well that I went out in the rain and got it all over again. Don't mention all this, please. I don't know what to think of it all.

Despite TWL's hopes, the Prohibition Era sorely tested AL, his wisdom regarding "the business of life."

AL to TWL
North Haven, September 1926

Dear Father,

As you may have heard, I loaned the *Penguin* (ed. to two college pals who wished to take the Lamont's family sailboat down east along the Maine coast as far as New Brunswick just across the Canadian border). They got as far as St. Andrews, stayed there a few days and started back, carrying with them a few bottles of whiskey, some for themselves and a bit for me. At Jonesport, customs officials boarded them and asked if they had any liquor. They answered "yes" and gave up the liquor. I knew they were going to bring back a little; in fact, I asked them to bring me some. The next day the officials came out again and said they would have to confiscate the boat—which is now in Rockland. I am very sorry this has happened . . .

TWL to AL
New York City, September 23, 1926

It was fine of you to take on your shoulders the blame for the whole *Penguin* expedition. To tell the truth, I have been a good deal concerned, not so much about the matter of possible publicity (which of course would have been deplorable) but because of the facts involved. Things are getting to a pretty pass when young college boys, no matter who they are, can't go down east without going into the bootlegging business. So far as you are concerned, I wish you would cut it out.

Queen Marie of Rumania was one of the more exotic foreign visitors to New York in the Twenties. She was lionized at parties as well as in verse (Dorothy Parker). TWL was beguiled by the Queen.

TWL to EAL
New York City, October 26, 1926

I was placed next to her at a luncheon last Friday, and to my surprise found her charming and delightful.[1] I asked her whether she wanted to talk seriously or lightly, and she said "Oh, lightly by all means." So I asked her to give me her views on bobbed hair and about how it felt being a queen—if she had her choice to live her life again, would she be a queen or just a plain person like the rest of us. She replied that, on the whole, she preferred to be a queen. She said that of course it had a lot of drawbacks, but that she got a lot

[1] In fact, Marie Alexandra Victoria was no slouch. She had shown remarkable spunk in World War I, working for her nation, and was the author of several books.

of kick out of it. I asked her to tell me a little about the Rumanians and whether it was a good language to make love in. She gave me a languishing look and asked me what I thought. Of course, you know she has a reputation for having had a number of affairs herself . . .

It was okay for CL to have polished off a bottle of grape on the Naples-Rome express a couple of years earlier, but when AL broke out the hard stuff, returning to Harvard on the New York-Boston run, his father finally ran out of patience.

TWL to AL
New York City, January 1927

This gossip about your taste for good liquor floated to your mother's ears the other evening and distressed her terribly. The rumors have been persistent about your swigging from a bottle of whisky, rum or gin all the way up, in a smoking compartment, from New York to Boston . . . also about the maintenance of a small bar in your room for the assistance of visiting "Porkers"[1]. Some months ago I found a note from you to Metcalfe, asking him to fix you up a thermos of cocktails for a journey. I mentioned none of this to your mother. Now, I don't kick because a boy drinks an occasional cocktail at a party or dinner. But the idea of its going so far as to cause constant gossip is intolerable.

[1]"Porkers", i.e. members of the Porcellian, AL's undergraduate club at Harvard.

FCL's and TWL's winter excursion to the Caribbean was for FCL, mercifully, a one-shot visit—that, despite J.P. Morgan Jr. having lent them his yacht.

FCL to CL
Yacht Corsair, February 1927

Yesterday we landed at Saba. There we found waiting donkeys & two chairs with long poles through them so they could be carried by two men each. Ole and I took the chairs, the men took the donkeys, and we began to climb the almost perpendicular trail. Every man, woman, child, dog, baby and donkey was out to greet our procession. The men all stopped work for the day. They followed us in crowds wherever we went.

We stopped two days at San Juan . . . too Americanized. Americans seem to have a genius for crushing out all the old civilization. I wonder if it really is impossible to be sanitary and picturesque at the same time.

FCL to AL
New York City, March 1927

Oh, it's so good to be home. I never was so glad to get home before in my life. Between you and me, I *loathed* the tropics. Thank heaven, I never shall have to go again . . .

That spring the Lamonts rented a house on Long Island, seeking respite from, yes, urban creep.

FCL to AL
Oyster Bay, Long Island, New York, May 1927

Englewood is so noisy and ugly. Here it rests my spirit just to look off into the woods with their tender green leaves just beginning, nothing to hear but the thrushes. If only Father would love it and consent to live here. Saturday and Sunday afternoons Father took me in his little car for a joy ride, and we went over back roads with cherry and pear trees all in bloom, and hardly met a car, everything woodsy and wild.

Later in the year TWL, sans FCL, was back in Japan. He and his bank had reached the peak of esteem there, having expedited a massive loan to Japan to get the nation back on its feet after the devastating earthquake of 1923. No fleabag hotels this trip. The Japanese gave TWL the full red-carpet treatment.

TWL to AL
S.S. President Pierce, enroute from Yokohama, October 31, 1927

The attentions showed to us were on a bewildering scale. Apparently they had laid careful plans to play me up as a national hero. The day I arrived in Yokohama many of the shops carried big lithographs of me designated as one of the saviours of Japan. Troops of school children were halted in the street and bowed down as I passed. The mayor of Yokohama sent me a beautiful blue and white porcelain jar as a gift.

Lavish luncheons and dinners were given in TWL's honor, attended by geisha girls galore and performances of the classical No dance. Crowds in the street shouted, "Banzai, Lamontosan!" At the old capital of Nara one morning, the mayor staged a special calling of the deer for TWL, and hundreds of Bambis came scampering out of the forest to be fed. The show in Kyoto really set TWL agog—a mushroom hunt in the woods at which TWL and his party were cheerfully assisted by a score of geishas imported for the occasion. TWL noted:

One of them was an especial beauty (in the American, not the Japanese style). She had been brought from Nagoya, a hundred miles away, for my benefit, and at dinner that evening she nestled at my feet and served me all I thought I dared eat or drink.

Before he left Japan, TWL had an audience with Emperor Hirohito whom he sized up as a young man with "heavy eyebrows" and "protruding lips." TWL also observed the official standing closest to the Emperor, a naval officer named Yamamoto, "a very jolly Japanese admiral" who acted as interpreter. Fourteen years later, the jolly admiral would mastermind the attack on Pearl Harbor.

Back to earth, TWL had to endure family cut-ups at Sunday church in Englewood.

FCL to AL
New York City, December 1927

We horribly disgraced ourselves with the most virulent attack of the giggles. The collection plate was passed. Corliss and Charlie Poletti[1] sat on one side of the aisle, and Pa on the other. When the plate came to Corliss, he fumbled in his pocket for some change and found only nickels. The solemn man with the plate stood there, everybody

[1]Charles Poletti, Lieutenant Governor of New York and an old friend of the Lamonts.

in church watching with interest. Corliss frantically pulled out his bill case and, meaning to put in a dollar, put in $10. At Corliss's expression of frozen horror, we all began to giggle and couldn't stop. Just as Eleanor and I sobered down, the pew rocked back and forth, and then we knew Corliss and Charlie were laughing, so we'd begin again. Father scowled in vain.

TWL to TSL, CL & EAL
S.S. Laurentic, January 1928

Tomorrow we land at the Prudential Life, formerly known as Gibraltar, and motor over for luncheon at Algeciras in Spain. At Gibraltar your Mother hopes to replenish some of the many articles of her wardrobe which she left behind.

On one of their last grand trips of the decade, TWL and FCL headed across the Atlantic, bound for Egypt via Madeira, Gibraltar and Naples. In Egypt TWL would meet with King Fuad ("the only man I ever met who could speak as bad French as I could and still make himself intelligible") and discover to his relief that the flies were "persistent but not vicious", the fleas "vicious but not persistent."

On the whole, the voyage has been very restful for everybody except your mother who has found the noises new and unfathomable. They are only the ones usual to giggling girls and shouting Shriners, and I think she will gradually absorb and assimilate them into the throb of the screw and the swabbing of the decks, to which on other voyages she has become accustomed.

Today the Captain and Chief Engineer did me the honour of taking me on an inspection tour of the machinery from boat deck to hold. It took three-quarters of an hour in 152° Fahrenheit, or thereabouts, and left me a limp rag. You know my love of machinery. I can't tell a condenser from a reciprocator.

FCL to AL
S.S. Laurentic, January 1928

This is the horridest boat I have ever been on, so noisy you can't sleep more than a couple of hours a night. The boat is managed by lunatics and built by morons. I am right under the bar, so I get my full share of all that's going on. Whenever anyone in the next room uses the wash basin, the pipes in my room give a quick succession of pistol shots that make me jump nearly out of bed. Last night there was a drinking party in one of the cabins lasting until 4 a.m. I shall be glad to get off this ship tomorrow at Naples. It is the worst trip I have ever had.

FCL's phobias were few but fixed. In addition to vacationing Shriners, she detested Broadway musicals, the military, and crossword puzzles. Of the last, she wrote CL, "I regard the habit as I do drink, opium smoking, or munching chocolates." Even the congenitally cordial TWL had a private exasperation or two.

TWL to AL
S.S.Laurentic, January 22, 1928

The Tildsleys[1] are good traveling companions, kind and unselfish. But Jack T has a supreme contempt for my banking capacities. He examines me carefully at breakfast each morning. "How many grams in a gold dollar, Tom?" "I don't know, Jack." "How much does a twenty-dollar gold piece weigh?" "I don't know that either, Jack." "I should think you would need those things in your work," says he. "No, I don't," say I, "but if I did, I would ring a bell and get someone to tell me." "Ah," says he, "but that wastes time and isn't like getting things first-hand, is it?"

[1]The John Tildsleys, old friends.

He thinks I spend my days like the old Fugger bankers[1] or the Venetian merchants, sitting in a little room and weighing out gold.

Enroute to Egypt, the Lamonts got word that FCL's aged father had died. "To lose a parent," TWL wrote TSL, "breaks one of the links that hold you to earth. No matter how many new ones you may have forged, they are not just like the old. Grandpa was always fine to me, took great pride in my modest goings-on. When I told him I wanted to marry your Mother, he said all right—'I hope you love her. Anyway you'll never have a dull moment'."

FCL to CL
S.S. Homeric, March 1928

I had the immense satisfaction of telling an American admiral over luncheon just exactly what I thought of the Naval program. We were both quite furious and quite determined, and neither of us ate a morsel. His reason for wanting a big navy is simply unbelievable, a disgrace to our country. Then he let off some pleasantries about the League of Nations, not realizing it was my pet hobby, and I was able to trip him up & knock him down & sit on him. I will say he remained polite and pleasant (ed. and, as history later proved, on the right side of the naval argument).

FCL to AL
New York City, Spring 1928

Pa had a party Saturday night. Dinner was at 7:30 and at 11 o'-clock it was still going strong. Father had Metcalfe show his moving pictures of Egypt. It was awful. Metcalfe couldn't get the focus

[1]The House of Fugger, a 16th century-family of German merchant princes.

right . . . Sunday I went to the new place[1], morning and afternoon. It is so beautiful, though we have to wear leather puttees if we go in the woods to protect us from copperheads. I can see where I step off to Jerusalem, my happy home. It has been revealed to me that I shall probably die in 1941—if not then, then I shall live till I am 92.

FCL to AL
New York City, April 1928

I have just come back from Milton[2]. Eleanor wanted me to stay there, at the Milton Hill House, so I did—the most uncomfortable place I ever struck. No food, no service, no water running in the bathtub, no blankets, no man to carry up your suitcase, or carry it down, millions of aged females, and the temperature at 110°. But I did enjoy seeing Ellie alot.

EAL to TWL
Milton Academy, May 1928

I think it's great that you're going to speak at graduation. Gosh, there's nothing to get nervous about in front of a lot of weeping graduates and stupid parents (Mr. and Mrs. TWL excepted). Miss Goodwin said that Mother suggested citizenship as a topic, and that sounds OK. But for heaven's sake, tell a couple of funny stories.

TWL to EAL
New York City, May 2, 1928

I am so glad to have your further suggestions in regard to my little talk at Milton on June 15th. Gosh, how I dread it! Of course, I hate to pull a long face, and furthermore I don't know anything serious to say. I asked Elizabeth Morrow[3] what they usually talk about,

[1]FCL and TWL had recently purchased a weekend home with 200 acres in rustic Palisades, New York.
[2]Milton, Mass., where EAL was in her senior year at Milton Academy.
[3]Mrs. Dwight Morrow, author, wife of the Morgan partner and U.S. Ambassador to Mexico; FCL's old Smith College friend and Englewood neighbor.

EAL and TWL at a wedding in Englewood, N.J., ca. 1928

and she said they usually talk about being on the threshold of life, with the portals opening out, all that sort of thing. She rather made me feel I didn't want to dwell much on this blah-blah stuff, although that is what you are now advocating. However, don't worry about it . . .

FCL to AL
New York City, June 1928

I'm just getting normal again after my strenuous jaunt to New England. Eleanor's graduation was the first item. Father made a speech and sat on the platform with all the big ones. Ellie won a prize. Miss Goodwin said, "The prize for the best speech of the year goes to Eleanor Allen Lamont (Father is all smiles) for her talk on Al Smith (Father's face falls a yard)[1].

I motored from Boston to Northampton[2], a most lovely ride. But everything lovely stopped at Northampton. I had a little cell with no bed, no bureau, no washstand, no glass. There was one narrow cot in the corner, with the mattress an inch thick, which fell off at frequent intervals during the night. But that was nothing to my mental anguish, trying to be chummy with a lot of fat old women (my age) whom I had never known. No more reunions for me!

FCL to CL and ML[3]
New York City, June 1928

The Republican platform is abominable. I can't bear to vote for Smith because he is so wet, but I fear I shall have to. I am thinking of writing Hoover, telling him how badly I feel not to vote for him and the reason why.

[1]Gov. Alfred R. Smith of New York, the Democratic presidential nominee that year, running against Herbert Hoover. TWL thought Smith "not first-class".
[2]Northampton, Mass., home of Smith College.
[3]Margaret Irish Lamont, CL's new wife.

FCL to CL and ML
New York City, July 1928

My life has been awfully stupid and awfully busy, a great mass of details. One afternoon Aunt Anne[1] and I had a tea party on the *Reynard*[2] for a friend of Anne's, an Englishman named Wyndham Lewis[3] who is in the public eye just now. He has written a book called *Time and Western Man* which I understand is very irreligious. You would probably love it, Corliss. He was horribly conceited and hadn't brushed his teeth in ten years, a bad combination.

FCL to CL
New York City, July 1928

I have been working hard on the new place at Palisades. Father gets 24-page letters from Aunt Lucy twice a week. They always begin, "Dear Brother, I do apologize for never getting time to write you a letter." We start for Sky Farm tomorrow. We can hardly wait.

The family real estate was growing. In addition to the Manhattan townhouse and a hideaway "cottage" in Yeamans Hall, South Carolina, there was Sky Farm, the TWLs' summer Xanadu on the heights of North Haven, Maine, with a panoramic view of Penobscot Bay. By the end of 1929 they would take up permanent residence on weekends in a country manor atop the Hudson palisades, some twenty miles upstream from Manhattan, with spectacular vistas of the river. They also bought a bigger yacht to replace the old Reynard, *this one a sleek, 75-foot-long craft of the same name, with a crew of five and mahogany paneling in the*

[1]Anne Parrish, the writer, FCL's sister-in-law.
[2]The Lamonts' first motor yacht, named after Masefield's famous narrative poem, *Reynard the Fox.*
[3]Wyndham Lewis, British writer and post-impressionist painter.

cabins. The new Reynard *ranged from the Hudson to the waters of Pulpit Harbor below Sky Farm, where even Metcalfe the butler kept a small yacht of his own, a 30-foot launch called the Royal George. Grandchildren, meanwhile, had arrived on the Lamonts' doorstep. FCL appointed herself Chief Babysitter in Residence.*

FCL to CL and ML
North Haven, Summer 1928

I am being head nurse and I work nine hours a day, but I love it. The only book I have read in a week is *Jack the Giant Killer.* The only sail I have had is on a painters' "horse" with a broomstick for handle and little Tommy for captain—pirates, of course. Do you know how hard it is to get little boys to eat their spinach at lunch? It requires diplomacy, force, imagination, a combination of Shakespeare and Napoleon. Well, that's me. I have a bad case of megalomania every day at half after noon. You can see me emerge from the battle tired but triumphant. After this, *anything* will seem easy. I could run Hoover's campaign for him.

FCL to CL
North Haven, Summer 1928

Thanks for the nice letter.

Corliss, it shocked me. You say the happiness of life is made up of various immediate enjoyments. I deny it. Of course, immediate enjoyments are good, but the big compelling ideals are better. To work for some chosen ideal, to bring it to pass in spite of disappointments and all sorts of hindrances—ah, that is worthwhile. The joy of the scientist when at last he proves his theory; the joy of the artist in his creation of beauty; the joys of the mother who, after long and hard work, sees her child developing with grace and nobility—ah, those are the things worthwhile.

Do you suppose the scientist on the last lap of his discovery cares whether he has immediate enjoyments, has beer or no beer? Not that the immediate joy of each day is not important—of course I think that—only that you cannot say there is "nothing else worthwhile in

The TWLs' yacht *Reynard*

life" or that "all our efforts should be directed to increasing the number and quality of the immediate enjoyments of all the humans in the world." It is much more important to give the humans an ideal than it is to give them a glass of Moselle. The highest thing of all is to give them faith in God.

But I am going to vote for Al Smith, I think.

In a similar trumpet call from on high, TWL had advised AL that, "The world is filled with millions of mediocre minds. We have to look to our best minds to take the leadership and bring the world along. Even though you are young, I think there is a heavy responsibility resting on you to do your share towards your fellows and the world generally. Fortunately, you will be so fixed that you won't have to scratch gravel to earn your daily bread . . . "

FCL to AL
Hyde Park Hotel, London, October 1928

Today, Tuesday, a luncheon at Sibyl's[1], and before that, a call from R. Nichols[2]. He gave me a series of recitations from his new play. He recited in a *very* loud voice and flung his arms about. At one point he fell on his knees and grovelled on the floor in front of me. At that instant, the door flew open and a bell boy appeared, looked scared to death, and fled.

FCL to AL
R.M.S. Mauretania, October 1928

It seems to make all my fellow countrymen wild with fury that I am voting for Al Smith. An old man asked me to tell him why and I was trying to explain very calmly, when suddenly he leaned forward,

[1]Sibyl Colefax.
[2]Robert Nichols, British dramatist.

almost shook his fist at me, and shouted, "I want you to know that my son was killed in the war!" No rhyme or reason, but very unpleasant. He is a Mr. Herman Clapp of Boston, and the Kinnicutts say he is crazy.

Adding injury to insult, FCL's candidate was badly beaten on election day by Hoover, TWL's choice. Ever magnanimous, TWL confined his joy to recounting a lame political joke.

TWL to AL
New York City, November 15, 1928

The day after the election a man was arrested in Richmond, Virginia, and charged with corruption: accepting bribes at the polls. The Judge told him the offense was a serious one and that he'd fare badly unless he made a clean breast of the whole story. "Well, Judge," said the man, "I was walking along the street when I met the Republican boss who handed me $5. A little later I met the Democratic boss who gave me $2. Then I went to the polls and voted." "Well," said the Judge, "how did you vote and why did you vote as you did?" "Well, Judge," said the man, "I voted for the Democrats because they seemed to me less corrupt that the Republicans."

FCL was glad to resume more matronly duties.

FCL to AL
New York City, November 1928

Little Tommy[1] has just started kindergarten. I saw him after the first day and asked him how he liked it. He said solemnly, "I saw

[1]Thomas W. Lamont II, first son of TSL.

Jesus." I was frightfully startled and wondered if we had a budding mystic in the family. But he added, rather condescendingly, "It's only a picture, Grandma."

FCL to AL
New York City, November 1928

Eleanor[1] has just telephoned that she swallowed some broken glass the night before last. So the family is not in its most hilarious mood.

FCL to AL
New York City, November 1928

I am just back from a short visit to Northampton. It is quite a long motor ride. Eleanor was in great shape. It seems to be a real tonic for her to eat broken glass. She is sowing her wild oats and enjoying it hugely. She lives on black coffee and bread, she wears no clothes, she wears thin canvas sneakers in the rain, she sits up till midnight every night studying because she spends all day writing love letters.

I arrived at Northampton Wednesday night. Ellie met me and said she couldn't have dinner with me as she had to be initiated at 6 p.m. into "The Orange and Black". She had to sit on a bench out in front of the hotel, blindfolded. I stayed with the poor creature. It was bitterly cold. They never came for her till 7 o'clock. She was freezing. I was so angry I nearly burst—and of course there was no one to blow off at without disgracing Eleanor. If ever I get an Orange-&-Black at my mercy!

FCL to AL
New York City, December 1, 1928

There isn't much news from Northampton. Ellie has had her hair bobbed, and the replies for her coming-out party invitations are coming in thick & fast. All the little girls have accepted, all the little boys

[1] EAL had begun Smith College that fall.

have declined. Ye Gods, what shall I do? If only I live until the 9th of December, which is doubtful, I shall be the happiest woman.

By the dawn's early light the morning of December 9th, so TWL later reported to AL in England, it appeared that EAL's debut at the Manhattan townhouse had been a crashing triumph, if a bit on the dry side. TWL's efforts to spice up the fruit punch with some of his prewar Bacardi rum had been nixed by FCL. They'd compromised by instructing Metcalfe to put in just enough rum to give the punch a hint of taste. One of the guests, remarking on the lack of wallop, said it must have been put in with "an eye dropper." The only booze at the TWLs' next party, New Year's day, turned out to be seriously medicinal.

TWL to AL
New York City, January 4, 1929

Your Mother decided it would be pleasant to play charades and to act out the words *Betty Morrow*[1]. The first word—*bet* and *tea*—were not difficult to act. For the first part of Morrow, Judge Hand[2] suggested acting Othello and Desdemona, on the theory that people would guess the word *Moor* which was enough like *Mor-* to make the first syllable. Faye Lippmann[3], a very beautiful young woman, was elected to play Desdemona. She lay down on a comforter on the floor, and Mary Hand's rather massive father came in and smothered her. He pounced on her with a pillow, and after the play was over she staggered to her feet with a heavy nosebleed. We took her upstairs, and I noticed that her nose seemed crooked. She was in great pain and almost fainting. We gave her some brandy, then I got hold of Dr.

---

[1]Elizabeth (Mrs. Dwight) Morrow, a guest at the party.
[2]Learned Hand, the distinguished Federal judge, often called "the tenth justice of the Supreme Court".
[3]Mrs. Walter Lippmann.

Poole in double-quick time. He found that her nose had been badly broken. He set it right away and we're in hopes her beauty will not be marred. Judge Hand felt dreadfully. He fears that for the rest of his life his career as a United States Judge will be dogged by the fact that he went to a party and broke a lady's nose.

FCL to AL
New York City, January 15, 1929

Our big news is about Father's going over to Europe as Mr. Morgan's alternate on the Reparations Commission. It's a big piece of work and I suppose the most interesting job in the world for a financier. I can't bear the thought of being in Paris two months, but I don't tell Father so. I hate Paris. After I've spent all my money on clothes and eaten myself into a bilious attack, there is nothing else to do.

It fell to TWL, as a key member of the American delegation to the Commission's conference in Paris, to carry the brunt of the negotiating over the issue of German reparations payments from World War I.

TWL to AL
Paris, March 8, 1929

I knew German Reparations would be engrossing, but I never thought they would knock completely out of my mind your 24th birthday, and I apologize.

FCL to TSL
Paris, March 1929

I did too much and have had a second attack of the flu, much more severe than the first. I am still in bed and very downcast. Father is working hard, but I do not believe he knows what it is to be really down-and-out physically tired. He is a sort of superman that way. There's no doubt in my mind that he ought to have two good, strong husky wives to spell each other. I'm all for polygamy.

TWL to CL
Paris, May 10, 1929

There is an old couple here who always come to Paris this time of year and whom I avoid more and more. She is quite deaf and therefore always speaks very loudly. At dinner in the Ritz grill the other night she came up to me and, after shaking hands, yelled, "Mr. Lamont, I wish you would get out of my bed! You have been in it now for almost three months!" Then, in a much lower tone so nobody could hear, she added, "My husband and I always had that apartment which you are in, and I think it mean of you not to adjourn the conference and let me have it."

CL in Munich, 1928

TWL finally yielded the apartment in June after the negotiations ended on a triumphant note. The press was so ecstatic over the American delegation's performance in Paris that New York Mayor Jimmy Walker offered to give TWL and his colleagues a tickertape parade up Broadway. The offer was politely declined.

FCL to AL
Englewood, September 30, 1929

Corliss showed me a letter he wrote you, in which he accuses me of arguing on behalf of the supernatural. Well, it all depends on what you mean by the supernatural. I mean by the supernatural the fact that there's more in reality that can be summed up in what our five senses tell us of matter in motion. When I argued for devils, I had in mind the fact that almost every belief that has been held deeply & passionately for long periods of time probably has some core of truth in it. All folklore and mythology of primitive peoples show this. So I believe that witches & devils have an underlying truth which can be interpreted in various ways.

Did I write you that Ramsay[1] is coming to dine at our house? But, alas, it is only a men's dinner. However, I am to receive them and I shall listen at the keyhole afterwards.

TWL to AL
New York City, October 14, 1929

Last Thursday the Prime Minister came to a dinner at the city house, which I arranged for him. Your mother received the guests and then retired. I had to meet men like Senator Root[2], Owen Young[3],

---

[1]Ramsay MacDonald, Prime Minister of Great Britain.

[2]Elihu Root, 84, long retired from a distinguished public career.

[3]Owen D. Young, Chairman of General Electric Co., had chaired the Reparations Conference in Paris.

John W. Davis[1], John D. Rockefeller, Jr., and a few others of that kind. (ed. There were 16 notables in all at the black-tie affair, including the president of Columbia University, Nicholas Murray Butler).

Margaret and Corliss attended a dance given for Miss Ishbel MacDonald[2]. Corliss danced with her three times and said she danced very well, so now I guess it's "Ishbel" and "Corliss". Last week also I had to go to a dinner given for those two prominent Britishers, Lord Birkenhead[3] and Mr. Winston Churchill[4]. Churchill quoted Virgil alot and rather abashed me by saying that his neighbor on the left (me) was the only other person who understood Virgil. In his speech he rattled the cerebrum a bit, speaking in rather an heroic vein. So when he sailed the next day, I sent him a box of cigars with the message "arma virumque cano"—to which he replied, by wireless, "arma feminasque ambo animus."[5]

FCL to AL
New York City, October 1929

Father tells me he has written you about Ramsay, so my ardour is rather dampened. Father wanted me to go downstairs to receive the men. So I did, and had my reward, as Ramsay came 15 minutes early, and the others 15 minutes late. So I had a lovely talk with him about peace, Spinoza, and bluebells.

During dinner I went down and stood behind the dining room screen to see how things were. The food was grand, the conversation seemed dull. But after dinner I listened from behind the drawing room tapestry while the men asked Ramsay questions, and it was thrilling. He talked enthusiastically and passionately. He thinks the

---

[1]John W. Davis, Democratic candidate for President in 1924.

[2]The Prime Minister's daughter who had accompanied him to New York.

[3]Frederick E. Smith,1st Earl of Birkenhead and the former Lord Chancellor.

[4]Winston Churchill, then Chancellor of Exchequer, had been deeply involved in war-debt matters.

[5]TWL: "I sing of arms and a man." WC: "We both sing of arms and women." (ed. with apologies to Virgil's *Aeneid*.).

old ways of security and protection have failed, and now we must try a new way, the way of the outlawry of war, of the Kellogg Pact.[1]

It seemed too good to be true, too amazing, that Ramsay could in all seriousness be saying that a new day had dawned, that war must go—and that sixteen of the leading men in America were listening and agreeing. It seemed as if the old Christmas carol had come true, that Peace should cover all the world, her ancient splendors fling,

And the whole earth gave back the song
That now the angels sing.

I was thrilled to my bones.

There was a big reception given by the Foreign Policy Association to which I went. I was selected to guard "Ishbel". Two thousand people went by the receiving line and I was amazed at the number of utter fools there were. One woman leaned over to Ishbel and said, "It is so wonderful to see a natural-looking English girl," which infuriated Ishbel. She muttered to me, "I'm Scotch."

It was not a good year for optimists. There would be peace for another decade, yes, but not in the money markets. A good thing TWL was not a betting man. He who lived by the crystal ball in '29 ended up eating ground glass. TWL got a mouthful of it with his rosy economic predictions. Still, when the Crash came he did all he could, as leader of the bankers' emergency-response team, to stem the panic selling on Wall Street. Time Magazine saluted his efforts by putting him on its cover.

FCL to AL
New York City, October 1929

The panic in Wall Street has been simply terrible. Father has been magnificent and has added enormously to his prestige. I called up Mr.

[1]The Kellogg-Briand Pact, signed in August that year, resolved to ban war as a means to settle disputes, substituting, instead, diplomacy and world opinion.

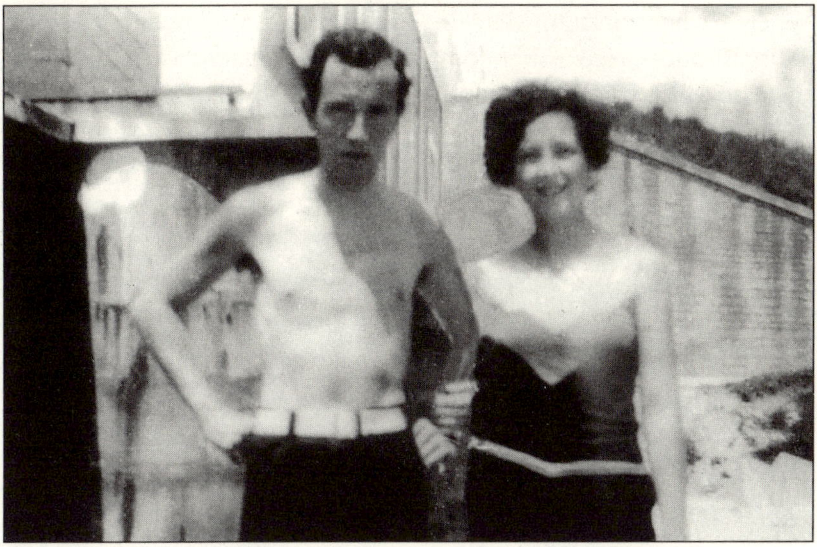

AL and EAL at the Lido, Venice, ca. summer 1929

Sanders[1] on the worst day to see how things were going and how Father was. You know how high-minded Mr. Sanders is. He said, "Oh, Mr. Lamont is doing noble work. All the financial world turns to him. Why, Mrs. Lamont, he's not even trying to save his own fortune at all, but only other peoples'!" I said, "How horrible, Mr. Sanders. Do tell him to save some of his own."

I shall never again go big with Mr. Sanders. He was so disappointed in me.

FCL to AL
New York City, November 1929

One night I was just starting out to dinner, when I picked up the evening paper and saw "GIRL KIDNAPPED AT SMITH COLLEGE" in large letters. Of course, I knew it was not Ellie. But I felt troubled and asked Metcalfe to call up & see if she was safely in for the night.

[1]The Morgan bank officer who supervised the Lamont family account.

When I came in later, Metcalfe had typed the following message: "Miss Eleanor presents her compliments to Madam and begs to state that she weighs 145 pounds and is well able to take care of herself."

Enter the 1930s. In the debris of the Crash, Americans experienced the first extended period of economic curtailment in their history. Credit had collapsed, savings evaporated. Ordinary folk despaired of opportunity. The old civic religion of democracy and enterprise now seemed impotent, wrote one historian of the period. Millions longed to shut out their distress by reverting to older, simpler small-town virtues and biases. Others were tempted by alternative systems. Intellectuals were drawn to Communism, the hoi polloi to demagogues. A branch of the Methodists, the church of TWL's childhood, vowed to renounce the capitalist system. The fiery radio priest, Father Coughlin, condemned the "financial Dillingers" on Wall Street.

If the Lamonts' private world remained sheltered from the turmoil, their impact on the business and cultural scene was increasingly noted. TWL had begun to assume near-Olympian stature on Wall Street. He stood at the right hand of Morgan the Younger who, though nominally head of the bank, was so retiring and self-effacing that TWL shone by comparison. TWL thus emerged faute de mieux as the firm's dominant figure of the decade. His Morgan partnership had assured him, in the words of Frederick Lewis Allen, "a place on the general staff of what the business world considered the headquarters of financial power."

From this perch, observed another writer, TWL, more than any other person, exercised unparalleled power for twenty years in the western hemisphere. He had become by the Thirties the so-called First Consul de facto in the invisible directorate of postwar high finance and politics. Highly conscious of the imperial obligations which attended such power, he served among other things as unofficial mentor to President Hoover, much as he had to Woodrow Wilson in the latter's second administration. By 1932, TWL and his colleague Dwight Morrow were shuttling in and out of the White House "with the regularity of confirmed tipplers visiting their favorite tavern," as author Ferdinand Lundberg put it.

TWL had also become one of the more influential backstage forces in contemporary American journalism as a onetime newspaper owner, financial angel of the respected Saturday Review of Literature, and a reliable shaper of many of the eventful business stories of the day. He was the favored source of reporters who in those days were still relatively untutored in complex financial matters. He thus attained a sort of shadowy journalistic eminence, aided in part by one of his most important editorial outlets, Walter Lippmann. The combination—Presidential advisor, editorial opinion shaper—made TWL not only the indispensable Morgan partner but assured his natural entrée into the world of high literature and international politics. A later historian admired TWL's protean grace, "his ambition to lead a beautiful, rounded life and bring poetry into the straitlaced world of banking."

The frequent dinners hosted by TWL and FCL at their Manhattan townhouse included writers like H.G. Wells and André Maurois; playwrights and poets like John Galsworthy and Robert Frost; deep thinkers like Julian Huxley and Harvard president James Bryant Conant; political heavies like Lloyd George and Lord Halifax; even the occasional actor like Charlie Chaplin. The Lamonts' guestbook comprised a Who's Who of literary thank-yous: Arnold Toynbee wrote his out entirely in Latin; the novelist James Hilton appreciatively penned, "How blest the age when writers roam / three thousand miles and find—a home!"

TWL to EAL
New York City, January 7, 1930

Yesterday evening your Mother and I dined with Edna Ferber[1]. The Lippmanns were there and also Captain Cazalet, the youngest member of the British House of Commons. We all went to "Sweet Adeline". You know how your Mother hates musical comedies, and

[1] Edna Ferber, the Pulitzer prize-winning author, was still basking in the triumph of *Showboat*, her 1926 novel that had been transformed to the musical stage with vast success.

this was no exception. Your Mother says that not only will she never go to another musical comedy, but that she is not going to the theatre again unless it happens to be some first-night play like Robert Nichols' or something like that.

TWL to EAL
New York City, February 7, 1930

Yesterday your Mother and I went south and dined with President and Mrs. Hoover at the White House. It was a formal dinner, but I thought it was rather fun. Your Mother had a pleasant fight with Alice Roosevelt[1] on the question of the World Court.

FCL to AL
New York City, March 1930

Austey, do think seriously before you go to Corsica. It's a dreadful summer resort. Probably there are malarial mosquitoes. They could wreck your life.

FCL to AL
New York City, March 13, 1930

The new baby came last night. Everybody was here for a family party—Mimi, Tommy & Ellie, Corliss & Maggie, Mrs. Miner. They all went to the theatre except Mimi and me. Tommy & Ellie left the theatre almost at once, and before the theatre was over the baby had arrived—awfully quick work. Of course, everyone is disappointed that it wasn't a girl. Poor little boy, nobody wants him.[2]

---

[1] Alice (Mrs. Nicholas) Longworth, the gossipy, tart-tongued daughter of Teddy Roosevelt. She once told another dinner guest, "Young man, if you've nothing good to say about anyone here, come sit next to me."

[2] The unwanted Broadway baby was Lansing Lamont, FCL's and TWL's third grandson.

TWL to AL
New York City, March 17, 1930

The chief excitement of the last week has of course been the new baby. I gave a family party at the theatre that night to see a brand new play, "Green Pastures"[1]. Just before the curtain rolled up, I saw Ellie give Tommy a look, and then they both beat it for the hospital with Mrs. Miner after them. They don't know yet what they will call the new kid. They were all set for a girl to be called Helen.

That spring, after attending a financial conference in Brussels, TWL joined FCL in London. They lunched in May at Chequers with Prime Minister MacDonald. FCL shared her notes of the occasion with AL and CL.

After luncheon we (ed. FCL and the P.M.) walked up a lovely hill. I said, "It would be nice to sit under that tree and read the Testament of Beauty with you." He said, "Let's make a tryst." I said, "All right, two years from now." He said, "Oh, I hope I shan't be here two years from now. It is too difficult, too much responsibility." He seemed oppressed by his position. "It is so hard to make decisions and not know what will follow from them." I said, "Yes, a man ought to have a single vision and follow it like a steamroller." He said, "Yes, a man in my position should have no imagination." He was awfully interested in birds' nests and kept hunting for them in the hedges. Interested, too, in the landscape and in flowers. The forget-me-nots under the trees lay in great blue pools.

Then over to Cliveden[2]. Lord Astor feels that the naval conference did a lot of good. He blames the French a good deal. I took a little

[1] *Green Pastures,* by Marc Connelly, was the hit of that Broadway season.

[2] Cliveden, the Astor estate on the Thames, had become a favorite watering spot for Britain's leading politicians and intellectuals, some of whom later associated themselves with the appeasement cause vis-a-vis Nazi Germany.

walk with Philip Kerr (later Lord Lothian)[1]. He told me the story of a Mississippi man who saw the Thames for the first time. The Englishman who was with him said, to forestall any comparison with American rivers, "That, sir, is not a river. It is liquid history."

At luncheon the P.M. told an amusing story, illustrated with many gestures, about the Japanese man who drank too much brandy and kept trying to wipe his nose away. I felt that stories of that kind were not his metier. Altogether he is a sweet person, sensitive, imaginative, rather philosophic—a strange person to head a Labour cabinet. On the other hand, Tom Jones, the labour leader whom we met here at Cliveden, is hard as nails. I enjoyed a good scrap with him.

FCL's daunting Puritanism and constant quest for self-improvement had apparently infected CL. He declared his intention to withdraw from the summer pastimes of his siblings to devote himself exclusively to serious intellectual pursuits—a declaration that elicited a biting response from his mother. As always, like TWL, she preferred to transcend mere scolding, the better to examine a particular of the larger ethical life.

FCL to CL
North Haven, August 1930

It is hard for me to believe that you, with your keen sense of humour & your sanity, can really have developed a persecution complex. It is simply ridiculous to say that the pervading atmosphere at Sky Farm was "hostile" to you. No one really feels that you are "queer" & "snobbish" any more than we feel Eleanor is queer never to open a book or Tommy queer to play golf all day. We are all a little queer to each other. But your attitude of having fallen from grace, of having sinned because you occasionally went for a sail or played

[1] Philip Kerr, diplomat; secretary of the Rhodes trust, South Africa; formerly secretary to Prime Minister Lloyd George.

a rubber of bridge is amazing. Surely, you realize that it is wisdom and fullness of life, not knowledge, that we are all after. Knowledge is a means to an end. That end is wisdom. The traditional professor buried in his books, with no contacts with life, with no passions, has never been counted wise. If you are going to have contacts with life, what more enriching ones than with your family who adore you? Love is very developing.

I do not think it is true that I have discouraged you in your intellectual life. I am sorry that you have allowed yourself to fall so completely in love with the writing of John Dewey[1]. I should have liked you to have a wider knowledge of philosophy before you gave yourself heart and soul to one aspect of it, with utter scorn for all other aspects. I think the wise man is not so scornful and has a suspicion that truth is more widely spread.

I think, too, you have misunderstood my stand on academic freedom. I think everyone has a right to express his opinion freely. I think there are other rights, too, and sometimes the rights and duties conflict, and one has to choose between them. I am not sure that to express one's opinion is always the supreme right and duty of the moment. I think this covers the case for academic freedom.

FCL ended her sermon with an indignant swipe at CL's apparent suggestion that she might profitably adopt a mellower mode as she approached her twilight years.

My twilight years of timidity, compromise & hush-hushiness indeed! You bet your sweet life, there's no twilight about me. You never made a bigger mistake in your life. I am going to go on to the end in the bright sun like Jesus and Socrates. Even that dull old septua-

[1]Dewey's advocacy of pragmatism and social welfare, his distaste for abstract learning, probably didn't square with FCL's idealism and traditionalist approach to life.

genarian John Dewey is not any more twilighty now than he's always been. I think it's only those who believe in God who renew their strength like the eagles, and run without fainting.

A month later she couldn't resist tweaking CL for his over-earnestness.

FCL to CL
North Haven, September 1930

Bless you and the little new baby[1]. To think of your having a daughter, it's too wonderful. Father and I sat up late last night thinking over all the ways we should try to spoil her and make her frivolous. We have some fine plans that we will tell you of.

A year after the Crash, TWL was still too busy to take more than the occasional motor trip out of town.

TWL to AL and EAL
New York City, October 28, 1930

Ten days ago Corliss and I, your Uncle Jack and Aunt Lucy took an expedition upstate to visit, at Aunt Lucy's urging, my birthplace at Claverack, New York. Aunt Lucy was convinced she could remember perfectly the Methodist church and parsonage. So we motored to a church in the little village, which Lucy said was the right one, and the house next to it looked like a parsonage. Nobody was at home, but Corliss climbed up on the window ledge, saw a book lying in the library, entitled "Jesus for All", and concluded it must be

[1] Margaret Hayes, named after her mother.

the parsonage. So Uncle Jack took out his camera and photographed the house from various angles, this constituting in his mind important documentation. He also photographed the church until he had only one film left. We started to leave, when Aunt Lucy had a little doubt creep in her mind whether it really was the old parsonage. So she asked next door and found that both the church and parsonage were Dutch Reform. Uncle Jack was crestfallen.

Then we piked off to the other end of town where we were told the real parsonage was. This time I myself approached the house, and, walking around the front door, which seemed rather forbidding, I came on a woman who was carrying a pail of water. When she saw me, she dropped it and ran screaming into the house. I felt very apologetic and made my best bow to another woman who came out, and said I was sorry if I had frightened anyone. She said it was quite all right, it was only her idiot sister. Then she told me that this really was the parsonage where I was born. She said she would like to take me upstairs, but that if I went up her sister would have fits. So I begged off.

Undeterred, they motored over to nearby North Hillsdale where the first Lamont ancestor in America had been buried in 1786: Robert Lamont, TWL's great-great-great-grandfather. The gravestone was still legible, as were those of Robert's elder brother Archibald and his daughter-in-law Phoebe. The following month TWL sought to brace up his daughter who was having doubts about her junior year abroad at Oxford.

TWL to EAL
New York City, November 6, 1930

If you had spent this third year at Smith you no doubt would have got a lot out of it, but nothing such as you can get out of your time at Oxford. That means in breadth and outlook and a chance to establish a sort of intellectual standing place for yourself. You have, to

EAL sailing off North Haven, summer 1930

be sure, done excellent work at Chapin, Milton and Smith. But I am not sure you have ever reached the point where you feel your mental powers quicken and get the thrill of knowing that your mind is working like a fine machine and that with it you can accomplish almost anything within reason.

There comes a time when you must crave a wider range of thought and work. And that is just what you are coming to this year, if you are patient and resolved.

I was disappointed to realize that, at first, you took the change of environment so hard and seemed for awhile to lie down under it. Most people have enough real trouble—let alone taking as trouble the most wonderful chance a person ever had—establishing the real things of life: habits of thought and work that will stand by you all your life, that will make you an infinitely better wife and mother, that will enrich the coming years beyond all measure of imagination. You can ask any one of your three brothers if, from his own experience, that is not true, and he will tell you 'yes'. You need not reply that you are different from your brothers. Because in quality of mind you are just as good as any of them. All you have to do is use the same willpower and grit.

It's been panicky down in Wall Street. I have had to organize sudden rescue parties. But in the midst of it all, in the silent reaches of the night when it is sometimes hard to sleep, I shut my eyes and see your sweet face, and smile and am cheered and helped. I was reading last night an old letter that President Eliot of Harvard wrote years ago. He said, "But be sure that thinking, working and loving are the real sources of lasting happiness." That's all true, and there's no one in the world who has greater capacity for all three of those things than you, darling Ellie.

Your lovingest

Da

FCL to AL
New York City, January 1931

We have been intensely social, dinners, luncheons, all sorts of lovely people coming to tea. I am enjoying it all. After all, it's only one month out of the year when I do this. Our "Murder" party was a great success. Edna Ferber said, "Count me out, I hate games. I'll go sit in the dark & think." Then she played wildly and was the last to go.

TWL to AL
New York City, January 19, 1931

The Depression still continues. Yesterday I received a letter from a friend of mine to whom I had lent some money—not a very close friend, just an old school friend. And he said, "Dear Tom: I deeply regret that I am unable to pay back the money which I owe you, but I want you to know in what esteem I hold you. In my will, which I have just revised, I have named you as first among my honorary pallbearers."

The new electronic age continued to thwart FCL and TWL. Someone had once written about another mechanically challenged couple that "the world was a treacherous quicksand, and by bad luck the best they could bring to it was ineptitude and a trusting heart." Long before World War II produced Murphy's Law, its precursor had already wreaked its particular vengeance on FCL.

FCL to AL
New York City, January 1931

Last Tuesday at home I was going upstairs to have breakfast with a visitor when I suddenly remembered I hadn't powdered my nose. So I pressed the red 'stop' button and the elevator refused to budge. I shouted & shouted and finally got Metcalfe who went down in the subcellar to tinker with the machinery. I could hear him say to Joseph (ed. another employee), "Had I better touch that button?" "Oh, no, stop, that's dangerous!" "Well, shall I move the little wheel?" "I dunno." I was petrified they'd press the wrong button and the elevator would dash to the ground, and I'd be broken to bits. I was really terrified. I even prayed. Finally, they phoned the Otis Elevator people who, after ages, got a mechanic to release me. The moral is, Don't powder your nose.

That same afternoon I spoke on the radio. I was rather scared, but my voice carried very well. They told me I must fill 14½ minutes exactly. Then they cut me off in 13¼, so that all the end of my speech was shut out. I was furious. The blood all rushed to my head in great waves which beat and pounded. I thought I should die of apoplexy then & there. I shall never be angry again.

TWL found himself culinarily and etymologically challenged by Nelson, the Reynard*'s Norwegian steward and chef.*

TWL to AL
New York City, January 1931

Nelson is doing quite well with the cooking except desserts. All he can make is jello. He calls it "yellow" and it is awful. I said, "What are we having for dessert tonight, Nelson?" He said, "Yellow". "Yes, but yellow what?" "Just plain yellow," he replied. So I gave up in despair.

Hard times continued to plague the country that spring. Morgan the Younger, feeling guilty, decided to forego travel and temporarily mothballed his yacht Corsair. He told the Archbishop of Canterbury it was unwise "to flaunt such luxurious amusement in the face of the public." TWL, however, favored Montaigne's view that, "Relaxation and affability, it seems to me, are marvelously honorable and most becoming to a strong and generous soul." He assembled his wife, his personal staff, the classics scholar Gilbert Murray and the Walter Lippmanns for a cruise through the Aegean. They would explore the antiquities of Greece and sample some more vintage chaos at the hands of the locals.

FCL to CL
M/N Saturnia, April 1931

We are all reading up on Greece furiously. Every night we read out loud to each other. The smoking room thinks we are lunatics when it hears Thucydides come booming through the smoke. Every afternoon Pa and I play bridge with the Lippmanns. See how low your mother has fallen!

She could not forbear cautioning CL on his adamancy that socialism, not capitalism, was the answer to the world's troubles.

Do the next thing with all your might & main, work for it, sacrifice for it. But if it does not work, do not despair—there can be no one hard & fast program for all time. It *has* to be trial & error. You cannot lay down a plan for all time. We have to be experimentalists whether we like it or not.

Then TWL piled on.

TWL to CL
M/N Saturnia, April 3, 1931

This steamer is lovely but vibrates like a seismograph in Nicaragua.

As to our present system of economics and industry . . . nobody but a fool would claim it as approaching perfection. But isn't the question, Are we making steady progress in improvement? If, as I think, we are moving forward, is there a brand new method which will get us faster to the goal we all desire? I call socialism new, even though it be centuries old. You think it is a better and quicker way,

TWLs and guests on board the S.S. *Saturnia*, en route to Greece, 1931. First on left, Henry James, son of the philosopher William James; fourth on left, Professor Gilbert Murray; fifth on left, FCL; at head of table, Captain Stuparich of the *Saturnia*; fifth on right, Mrs. Faye Lippmann; fourth on right, TWL; second on right, Walter Lippmann.

but I don't. I don't think America will vote to adopt that method in even your time. Socialism is a wonderful ideal to discuss. But I don't think it has worked well or will work well in our community.

FCL to TSL, CL and EAL
M/N Saturnia, Nauplia, April 1931

Eye hath not seen, neither hath it entered into the heart of man to conceive, the beauty of Greece.

Except that FCL's and TWL's opening scene there was pure Marx Brothers. Or, as TWL recalled, "like an Anthony Hope novel." Their party had landed at Patras on a Wednesday evening.

TWL to Children
Le Petit Palais, Athens, April 17, 1931

The Governor of the Province; the Captain of the Port, in full gold braid; a representative of the Greek Cabinet; the American Consul and Vice Consul—all came dashing out to the steamer in a special tender, lined themselves up in formal array in the saloon, and tendered us the welcome of Greece. They insisted on sabotaging all the steamer's landing arrangements, despite our earnest entreaties, and in landing us and our 42 pieces of luggage before anything could happen. It was a struggle between the Governor and Metcalfe as to who should carry your Mother's bottle bag and hat box.

The Governor marched us up the quay to the hotel where they gave us a very decent dinner and proposed toasts to us—"The descendants of the ancient Achaeans to the modern Ulysses, etc., etc." (ed. FCL recounted the scene with a slight variation. Her personal maid Josephine had been almost in tears at the confusion, "all the other passengers glaring at us with hate as we made our quick getaway. When we landed, Father said in a lordly way, 'Let us go on to the hotel', and the poor Lippmanns obediently followed.")

After dinner it was discovered that two trunks were missing. Metcalfe was invisible. So I sneaked away and had myself rowed out in the midnight darkness to a lighter out in Patras Harbor. It was loaded with a thousand trunks and loose bed springs which acted as traps to catch you as you searched with matches through the swaying trunks. But I located the missing ones and got back undiscovered. The Greek Cabinet representative assured me the next morning that they'd taken extraordinary precautions for our comfort and that he himself, under government orders, had personally inspected all the toilets on our floor in the hotel!

Things improved, more or less. TWL and FCL survived the Greek country food (which friends had told them would be mainly rank goats' cheese and resinous wine). After visiting Olympia, they returned to Athens via a private train.

The Petit Palais has no elevators, but we are on the first floor so it makes no difference—except in your mother's room one has to devise an elaborate system of shoes hung on a hair-trigger, so that if a robber climbs a ten-foot wall to get in at the window, he will knock all the shoes off and create an alarm . . . This morning your Ma stepped into her bath, turned on the shower by mistake and absolutely ruined her permanent wave. There is nobody in all Greece who can restore it properly. What is the use of Parthenons and Hermes and everything in such a land?

After a short stay in London, TWL hurried back to New York to handle a financial crisis. FCL took a later ship home.

FCL to AL
R.M.S. Mauretania, May 1931

I have had a fine rest on this ship. I sit at the Captain's table and am bored to extinction. Nobody speaks a word except, occasionally, the Captain and I. Last night the dullness was broken by one of the girls coming down to the table dead drunk. I felt so grateful to her. She made quite a diversion. I am going to write her a letter of thanks.

In truth, going or coming, FCL's preferred shipboard pastime appeared to be seclusion. In a letter to the children, TWL claimed FCL spent almost all her time in bed, "getting rested for the literary and philosophical debauch" that awaited her on foreign shores. It was these "debauches" among the literati, principally English, that prompted CL to pen some doggerel to his mother during one of her despondent moods that summer:

"There was a swell lady named Florence
Who attracted young men by the torrents.
They called every day
And to get them away
She had to give looks of abhorrence.

But the ghost of Don Juan, D.L. Lawrence,
Absolutely refused to leave Florence.
He chased her one day
In an eth'real way
And she fell down the stairs in respondence."

FCL and TWL differed in their tastes for the good life. Vacationing in Bermuda in early 1932, FCL complained to her children about "the cheap noisy crowd" at their hotel, "doors slamming, elevators banging, mosquitos biting all night, and drunk Americans talking loud till all hours under my window." Then there'd been the boat trip down . . .

FCL to AL
S.S. Monarch of Bermuda, February 1932

Such a wild, devilish journey. It's been *very* rough ever since we left. The night was bad because I had to cling for dear life all through it to keep from being hurled out of my bed, and so couldn't sleep. After lunch, as I was coming up in the elevator, just as the door opened to let us out, the ship rolled way over and I was hurled out of the elevator and flung clear across the boat. I have a black eye and a sprained wrist . . . There is a druggists' convention on board, all uproariously drunk. But now, heaven be praised, they're all seasick and we can have a little quiet and rest. Every cloud has a silver lining.

TWL to TSL
Bermuda, February 11, 1932

I find my party a trifle old. A magnificent swimming pool here, sparkling water, and temperature perfect, but none of my party wants to go in. They stand around the edges like a lot of chickens and watch me go in all by myself. Then they want to dine at 7:30. I say, life doesn't come into the dining room till 9 p.m., and none of the gay ladies from Hamilton, wearing no stockings, turn up for the dancing till 9:30. I suppose I shall be old some day and like to go to bed at 10 p.m. But you can be young only once!

TWL aboard ship in 1930s

On his annual spring jaunt to Europe with FCL, TWL again found the shipboard company wanting.

TWL to AL
S.S. Ile de France, April 14, 1932

There are several vampish looking women aboard, but I find that it doesn't go much beyond the lipstick. They tame down when you meet them . . . Sybil Walker[1] and I fight quite alot about her bidding at bridge which is as wobbly as her dancing. In the latter she has no sense of time, and therefore dances better when the ship is rolling at a 45-degree angle. Secretary of State Stimson[2] is agreeable but solemn. His wife is pleasant, but no sense of humor.

The Captain gave us a grand dinner the other evening. He sat the dignitaries on either side of him and the wives opposite, below the salt, so to speak, or like Japan & China where wives qualify chiefly for breeding purposes . . . Then at 5 p.m. yesterday the Captain summoned us to the ship's concert and set us all down like a lot of blooming waxworks in the front row. A young man fluted a flute till he was black in the face, a violinist played Debussy (whom I don't understand), and a Spanish dancer danced. A huge Slovak or Georgian or Greek or something, in a dress suit, sang the *Volga Boat Song.* A young woman, quite pretty in a tight green silk evening frock from which she was bursting at every seam, straddled a large bucking bronco of a cello, scaled some precipitous heights with it, and came down just in time to keep her shirt & frock on. It was all very inspiring.

[1]Miss Walker, a family connection "who just sort of came along".
[2]Henry Stimson was enroute to a disarmament conference in Geneva.

The Lindbergh kidnapping that March cast a pall over the year for the Lamonts who were close friends of the flier's wife, Anne, and her parents, Dwight and Betty Morrow. At Palisades, not far from Hopewell, New Jersey, and the Lindbergh home, where the kidnapper had entered an upper window to snatch the baby from his bedroom, TWL and FCL made some unwanted adjustments. From then on, the carefree family walks and games of hide-and-seek that ranged across the manicured lawns were eyed discreetly by an armed watchman. Steel bars were installed across the grandchildren's bedroom windows.

FCL to TSL
Galen Hall, Atlantic City, New Jersey, March 1932

I think and live nothing but the Lindbergh tragedy. Although I have had far greater griefs, I think nothing so shocking has ever come into my life. Father and I went down to Hopewell last Saturday. We were the only ones of Betty's friends who have seen her, as Charles will not let people come to the house. The place is terrible, the most God-forsaken, forbidding, weird, lonely place imaginable. You know I always like lonely places, so when I tell you this place is dreadful, you can really believe it. Charles and Anne and Betty are unbelievably brave.

As 1933 debuted, TWL was in his 62nd year, FCL in her 59th. TSL, at 34, was a rising executive at the Morgan bank and the father of three small sons. AL, 28, was married and studying for his graduate degree in medicine at Johns Hopkins University. EAL was now ELC, a bride of barely six months in London with her husband Charles Cunningham who was preparing at the Courtauld Institute for a career in arts administration. The nation was still mired in the Depression, awaiting the

Palisades, New York, ca. 1940

inauguration of President-elect Franklin Roosevelt. CL, now 30, had just published his first book. He was becoming increasingly outspoken about the excesses of capitalism and its wealthier practitioners such as John D. Rockefeller, Jr. TWL responded, defending Rockefeller in homespun terms.

TWL to CL
New York City, January 5, 1933

. . . He himself has lived quietly and modestly, not having had even a *Reynard* to disport himself on. Years ago when you and your brothers were in school and college, and his sons were just entering school, he asked me about my practice as to private allowances—what limits had I placed upon the allowances given to you and the others. When I told him none, he was shocked. He said that he felt every American boy should be rigidly limited in his allowance, so that he thoroughly gained an understanding of the value of money and realized that he must not waste when there was so much want gong on around him.

Aunt Lucy Gavit was still in touch with the Great Beyond and busily transmitting messages from same.

TWL to ELC
New York City, January 26, 1933

The day before your Mother's serious operation (ed. abdominal surgery), your Aunt Lucy received through her automatic writing a message from your grandfather Corliss[1] to the effect that he was standing by his dear daughter, was cheering her over the rough

[1]FCL's father, Wilbur Fisk Corliss, had died five years earlier.

places, was invoking his blessing upon her, etc., etc. Now, of course, this sort of message, coming allegedly from the other side of the Jordan, might have given a nervous patient a little turn, indicating that the family were inclined to believe that the patient herself was close to the River's edge. Your Aunt Lucy, however, apparently feeling it would be a distinct encouragement, forwarded the message to your Mother who read it. Her only remark was, "I'm just glad Father didn't say he was expecting me in time for lunch tomorrow and would be sure to have creamed spinach."

In England that summer TWL and FCL visited the Masefields in Gloucestershire and Lord and Lady Astor at Cliveden. TWL found Nancy Astor bewitching, a self-invented aristocrat who'd been born in Virginia and married up. She loved trading gossip and political scuttlebutt with her guests. The Lamonts schmoozed with delegates to the London Economic Conference and partied in London with the Prince of Wales. Later they unwound for a month at a country house in Devon with AL and ELC and their spouses. It wasn't all roses.

FCL to TSL
Pinbury Park, Cirencester, Glos., July 1933

. . . A weekend at Cliveden, most amusing. There was a garden party for all the delegates to the Economic Conference. Cordell Hull[1] and Senator Pittman[2] were staying over the weekend. Father turned pale with anxiety every time I opened my mouth, even if I only said, "Please pass the salt." It was an awful temptation to say what I

[1]Cordell Hull, newly appointed Secretary of State, was heading the U.S. delegation to the conference.

[2]Sen. Key Pittman of Nevada, chairman of the Senate Foreign Relations Committee.

thought about the Investigation[1], but I bravely overcame it. Cordell Hull, when he was introduced to me, said, "I have known your noble husband for years." And when he said goodbye, he said, "I hope I shall someday know you better." So perhaps when Pecora puts all the Morgan partners in jail, Hull will intercede for you.

P.S. G.B. Shaw at a luncheon said to me, "When I got out of the auto that your husband had kindly had take me to the steamer in New York, I said to the chauffeur, 'My God, man, why doesn't Mr. Lamont buy a new car?' And the chauffeur said, 'Because Mrs. Lamont won't let him'." All the luncheon guests stopped eating and listened in awed silence.

TWL to TSL
The Moult, Salcombe, South Devon, July 21, 1933

Lord and Lady Astor gave a dinner last Tuesday night for the American delegates to meet the Prince of Wales. There were about sixty there. Senator Pittman was as tight as could be—he was the same down at Cliveden. Governor Cox[2] seems a pretty good fellow. He asked me to join him and the Prince on a sofa after dinner. "I tell you, your Royal Highness," he was saying, "I tell you these days we are apt to forget fundamental principles. We try one thing after another. How simple if we could just remember that we can never get a good straight long ball down the fairway unless we *pivot* with both hips!" The Prince, who had been discussing Anglo-American cooperation in an aimless sort of way, was startled, but agreed.

---

[1]The big story in America at the time was the Senate investigation in Washington, the so-called Pecora Hearings, into the practices of leading banks including J.P. Morgan and Company. The hearings were conducted by the chief counsel of the Senate Banking and Currency Committee, Ferdinand Pecora.

[2]James M. Cox, former governor of Ohio and Democratic nominee for President in 1920.

FCL to family
The Moult, Salcombe, S. Devon, July 1933

Here we are, installed in the Moult. We arrived on a pouring, cold afternoon. Tom said, "I suppose the weather is always like this." Austin said he was getting a steamer ticket for America the next morning. Nancy[1] was wrapped in gloom and ten overcoats. The house is unbelievably shabby and down at the heel. The cook is very lame and slow and over 80. The butler has no teeth, it is impossible to understand one word he says. Metcalfe sleeps in the attic and has to go up a ladder to get there. He bumps his head badly every time. The beds are awful. Ellie & Charlie arrived from London the same night we did, and Ellie was furious and ranting around like Lady Macbeth because Austin & Nancy had pre-empted the one & only double bed. Eleanor's little dog has the mange, and the only place he really likes is inside my bed, which is a great trial to me. In spite of everything we are all very happy.

CL was still piquing his mother for her gadabout ways. She fired back with both barrels.

FCL to CL
Salcombe, July, 1933

As for your saucy letter to me, I fumed with rage. My dear infant, I was engaged in working for the good of society before you were ever born. I can remember my first efforts with the Consumers League. But now I think I can accomplish more in other ways than working on committees.

[1]Nancy Sullivan Lamont, AL's new wife.

No. 1. You say, "Why don't you stop flirting with poets and write a poem yourself?" I never flirt, but I think it's far better to inspire a poet to write a fine poem than to write a fifth-rate one myself.

No. 2. Why do I not write a novel? Because there are far too many bad novels written as it is.

No. 3. Why don't I do something for the State instead of tea-ing with statesmen? Because that is the only way I can work efficiently for the State. To plant a liberal idea in the mind of, say, Senator Pittman, would probably accomplish more than serving on a League of Nations committee for ten years. I think I planted several.

I have just about finished reading *The Metaphysical Foundations of Modern Science.* I commend the end of it to you for thoughtful consideration. I really think that philosophically you have not a leg to stand on, all is sinking quagmire under you . . .

Yesterday we went for a picnic up on Dartmoor. The pink & purple heather in blossom and the near hills covered with heather against the vivid blue of the ocean and the pale blue of the distant hills was shatteringly lovely. It made me tremble with a sort of ecstasy. The moors are so vast, so solemn.

Much love to you and Margaret,

Your unashamedly debutante but devoted Mother

P.S. May I point out (in case you say, "How can you enjoy the moors when you think of the starving poor?") that all the starving poor were on the moors having a swell time, and the only way we escaped them was by climbing 1,738 feet.

FCL to AL
Bermuda, February 1934

Life was very amusing in New York before I came here. Aunt Lucy's spook party was fun. Did I write you about it? About my beau from heaven, tall, blond, bearded, who stands close beside me and is waiting for me? The medium saw him plainly. It is very exciting. When our car skidded, coming in from Palisades, was I scared? Everyone else was, but not I. I thought of the beau waiting for me on the Other Side and was calm as calm. The medium took one look

From left, CL, FCL, EAL, and her fiancé Charles C. Cunningham, 1931

at Father, and said, "You have a very violent temper." I am glad to have that man unmasked. But it made Aunt Lucy furious.

Pa and I went to the Governor General's here for luncheon. He is very profane and hearty. He wants England to give the U.S.A. Singapore for a naval base, and then England and America to unite against the world, have no tariffs between themselves, etc. I said, "But what would become of the poor French?" He said, "Let them go to the devil, miserable swine!", and banged the table so hard that a decanter broke.

FCL to AL
Bermuda, February 1934

The Governor General came to luncheon and again got talking about the French. This time he called them "putrid swine" and said that in the War they were in a "stinking funk". We had a birthday luncheon for Lady Cubitt[1]. Tom and I each wrote her a poem. After Tom read his, Lady Cubitt hurled herself upon him and kissed him. I thought he would be pinned and flattened and crushed against the wall by the impact of such an immense body, but he came through it all right.

Charles and Anne Lindbergh summered on North Haven on the Morrow estate just a cove or two down from Sky Farm. Their front lawn, rolling down to the bay, was Lindbergh's private airstrip.

FCL to CL
North Haven, Summer 1934

The big event in my life has been flying with Charles Lindbergh.

The first day I arrived I was exhausted & in bed resting, when Charles called up and asked if I would like to take a spin with him. It took me just three minutes to spring out of bed, dress, powder my

[1] Lady Clive Cubitt of the dynasty which made its fortune building London's fashionable Belgravia district.

nose and get to the car. His plane is tiny, just barely room for two in the cockpit. When the plane first leaves the ground and you're conscious of really soaring, it is one of the most thrilling of all moments. We flew up 4,000 feet and went over North Haven, and skirted Vinal Haven, out on the ocean towards Isle au Haut, then over the sea to Hurricane and the White Islands, and then home. Charles was disappointed because it was a little misty, so yesterday he asked me again and I was pleased as Punch. It was a marvelous clear day. We went up 6,000 feet all at once and saw the distant White Mountains & the Whole World . . .

One of the books P. Van D.[1] sent me is in the form of the ever popular symposium, and one chapter is on Communism. The man says: "Communism is, in the last analysis, rooted in an ultimate lie about the universe, the falsehood that the supreme and final reality is in economic forces. Christ says, on the contrary, that the ultimate and immediate reality is God: that the goal of human society is brotherhood." I think that expresses pretty well my objection to Communism. Here we are in this world of beautiful possibilities and spiritual realities, and all the Communists can find are economic forces and determinism. Whereas the universe is shot through and through with spirit.

One day that June, while marching in protest on a union picket line in Jersey City, N.J., CL was arrested and briefly jailed. His parents viewed the incident with mixed emotions.

FCL to CL
Pinbury Park, Cirencester, Glos., July 1934

I was terrified at first when I found that you had been arrested and had such outrageous treatment. I still feel it was unfortunate because

[1]Pitney Van Dusen, the theologian.

I cannot feel that you are having a restful holiday. I feel that this fuss & row & bitterness may prevent your working at topnotch next winter. I think you tend to sacrifice the greater for the less. Still, I am proud of you that you care for anything intensely enough to go to jail for it.

I can't help feeling that you ought, right in your prime of life, to be doing work of such great importance that you would not feel justified in interrupting it for peaceful picketing, no matter how good the cause. Of course, if your life work is to be an organizer of unionized labour, then all right to do picketing . . . If you go to jail, I will be there every visiting day with a basket of goodies. I will wear my best clothes and tell all the jailers how terribly proud I am of you, and give them splendid little talks about helping the working man & how they all ought to be doing it.

TWL to CL
London, July 12, 1934

We received your long account of the proceedings in Jersey City. To tell the truth, I was never very anxious about the whole matter because, with all due respect, at this distance the whole thing seemed rather unreal to me. This is not meant to imply for a moment any disrespect for the principles involved or for your determination to follow them through. But you almost had to ask to be arrested. The newspaper account sounded as if you could have walked up and down in front of the factory all day without molestation unless you were really disorderly or attempted to gather a crowd . . . I always have my reservations in cases like yours where the association is obliged to get a well-known name in order to exploit its principle thoroughly, and I think a person like yourself is bound in all fairness to be chary as to how he permits his name to be exploited.

TWL to CL
Paris, July 20, 1934

I have your interesting letter of July 10th together with the article you wrote for *New Masses.* I have read them both very carefully.

Of course, anybody who carries a large black-and-white sign, the legend on which splits the infinitive completely, deserves bad treatment. I don't wonder you were arrested.

. . . Your sarcasm as to the *Herald Tribune* will, I fear, be a bit lost, and besides, don't think for a moment that the account in the *Tribune* was any "subtle attempt", as you call it, for carrying out some settled policy. It was just a feeble attempt on the part of some poor cub reporter who probably gets a small salary, to be a little amusing. I used to try to do the same thing when I was a reporter. So don't lay it against the poor lad too much.

Seven months later, TWL and FCL were bound for Los Angeles by steamer via the Panama Canal. By now, TWL had become habituated to the lifestyles of the high and mighty, from the court trappings of the Emperor's palace in Tokyo to the beginnings of the imperial White House in Washington. Royals of all stripes sought his ear. The one influential culture TWL had not sampled was Hollywood's. He got his first taste of it when they reached California. TWL made a solo pilgrimage (FCL declined the honor) to the San Simeon eyrie of William Randolph Hearst, the press lord.

TWL to AL
S.S. Santa Rose, February 5, 1935

This is a long, slow lazy voyage . . . dull enough people not to excite you, not enough feminine beauty to bewilder you, tropic skies and blue-green seas. Your Ma's maid Bertha has had a facial and blossomed out in rouge and lipstick. Prior thereto, on the only rough day, she upchucked on Metcalfe and spoiled his best suit. Ma has a facial every day and looks like the petals of a June rose.

FCL to AL
S.S. Santa Rosa, February 1935

The intense heat of the tropics absolutely knocked me out. I haven't been able to sleep and feel simply rotten. The other night there was the inevitable fancy dress ball. Father went as a Cardinal, in his red dressing gown and a purple cape an old lady had lent him. He looked simply splendid and acted the part so well that I began to wonder if my children were illegitimate. He lost first prize by only one vote.

FCL to TSL
Santa Barbara, California, March 1935

Father went to the big ranch on the mountain yesterday to see the wickedest man in the world. It was 340 miles there and back, quite a ride. I was furious because Pa got there at 1 p.m. and his host never turned up until quarter of three, when they had luncheon. I think it was a foul way to treat Pa. But he doesn't seem to resent it. He thinks he had a satisfactory talk and I believe is glad he went.

Was he ever.

TWL to ELC
Santa Barbara, California, March 4, 1935

I had a great experience, entre nous, a vastly entertaining time. The place is like a glorified combination of the Arabian Nights, Granada, Versailles, Blenheim, and God knows what all . . . When you came to the Castle itself the magnificence was unbounded . . . Gothic tapestries on the walls, mille fleurs tapestries beyond compare in the billiard room. Italian primitives were as common as ping-pong balls, the side tables in the dining room groaning with the weight of old silver—tankards, trenchers, flagons, everything!

And what about me and Marion Davies?[1] There she was, cordial and smiling. She was the hostess and laid herself out to please. There

[1]Marion Davies, Hearst's longtime mistress and struggling film actress.

were half a score of other movie actors and actresses flitting about, the girls in day pajamas. I couldn't keep track of them all. And a lot of others, young men, lounging about in riding togs, waiting for the weather to clear, kissing each other 'good morning' quite casually, then settling down to backgammon or ping-pong or perhaps breakfast. They were all very polite and trying to entertain me. I was the only person out of 40 at luncheon who had been so old-fashioned as to arrive by motor. All the others came by plane.

After luncheon, I had a long private talk with Mr. Hearst[1].

CL was not amused by TWL's visit with Hearst, whom he judged a demagogic rightwinger. TWL responded that he would talk "to any dictator in Europe or gangster in America" if it would help the cause of his bank or lead to better understanding of his country's economic system. He had already met with Mussolini five years earlier (though Al Capone he'd avoided). Kings were more to his liking, in particular Britain's new and fatefully enamored young monarch, Edward VIII, a.k.a. David Windsor.

FCL to ELC and AL
London, June 1936

Last night we went to dinner at Lady Colefax's, and the King was there—a small intimate dinner—also Mrs. Simpson[2], and Pa sat next to her. I had a little talk with "Davie". I looked perfectly horrid. My white satin dress didn't set right and my tummy poked out in a shiny white little ball, and my hair was foul. Everybody else was very young and very smart. But I had a swell time and didn't get to bed till 3 a.m. About 12:30 a.m. Noel Coward arrived, and sat at the

[1]TWL sought to disabuse Hearst and his newspapers of their animus towards the Morgan bank, and to enlighten the publisher on the value and accomplishments of American financial institutions.

[2]Wallis Warfield Simpson, the King's passion and the talk of London.

piano and played & sang the most divine songs. Do you know "Don't Let Your Daughter Go on the Stage"?

TWL had an especially appraising eye for Mrs. Simpson. He noted in a letter to AL that,

Mrs. Simpson had on lovely ruby and diamond jewels which the King had given her—square-cut stones—a magnificent ring, a clip at her breast, shaped like a fan, the outer spokes rubies and the inner ones diamonds, and gorgeous earrings of the same. They say that jewels are the only thing that she will accept from the King. Careful girl, I'd say.

TWL to TSL
London, July 13, 1936

I am feeling very fit, though of course cross at times, like an ancient mongrel when years have come over him. With all their delightful qualities, the British are the most go-getting and nationalistic people in the world. They don't grind their own axe half the time, but 24 hours a day.[1]

TWL to CL
Paris, July 25, 1936

Yes, Mussolini does seem to have gone off the deep end[2]. Alas, if I had anything like the contacts with him that you indicate, I might make some impression on him. If I thought I could, I should certainly attempt it. Speaking to you privately, he seems like the

[1]TWL had encountered stubborn resistance from political leaders like Churchill when he raised the subject of Britain's outstanding war debt to the U.S.
[2]Italy had declared victory that spring over Ethiopia which it had invaded the previous October. Mussolini's fascist empire was now a fait accompli.

AL, ELC, NL (AL's wife) and FCL aboard ocean liner, ca. 1936

Gadarene swine headed for the precipice, although the catastrophe may be several years postponed.

The Lamonts were headed for Cape Town, South Africa, to visit their old friend Jan Christiaan Smuts, the former Prime Minister of that country, now Minister of Justice, and a distinguished world statesman.

TWL to AL
R.M.M.V. Stirling Castle, June 2, 1936

We have already struck the Cape rollers and are doing a lot of pitching. I don't think, from all I hear, that Johannesburg is filled with innocence. We are due to stop there with Sir Ernest Oppenheimer, a Jew whom we all know, the head of the gold fields company of deBeers, the great diamond syndicate. We have taken along our swell clothes to stay there, whereas with the Smuts we wear only sports things day and night. Your Ma is very keen on our projected stay at the Smuts Dutch farm out in the veldt under the stars. I was told in London that all these old Dutch farms were full of fleas, so I sent Metcalfe out and bought some Keating Powder, but I haven't told the news to Ma yet.

TWL to ELC
Grand Hotel, Lydenburg, Transvaal, July 3, 1936

We have a caravan of five cars, with Genl. Smuts[1] driving his own. He drives with his left hand, just as for so many years he held his horse's bridle with his left hand and shot with a rifle from his right. He doesn't often take both hands from the wheel at the same moment—only when we are going around a curve on a high mountain and he wants to point out the beauties across the valley.

[1]General Smuts had led the Boer forces in the Boer War (1899-1902) and had been a field commander in World War I.

We have Metcalfe and your Ma's maid along—not to do for us but simply as members of the family. That's the usual status out here for all white people, for only the Kaffir "boys" and girls are called servants. It is all very nice and simple, just as it should be. Mrs. Smuts is a bright and well-educated woman but a typical Dutch haus-frau. She calls the General "Papa" or "Oe' Baas", Old Boss, and trots around the house superintending everything. There are no indoor toilets, only an old wooden outdoor John. At times there is quite a run on the bank.

Mrs. S. was reading the other night from the paper—little girl in Port Elizabeth just died from the bite of a puff adder. "Ach, yes," says Mrs. S., "they climbed into our kitchen last summer, two of them, but the 'boys' killed them. You see, this house of ours is built on the site of an old native kraal, and there's a whole nest of poison snakes under the house. You wouldn't be afraid, of course." "Oh, no," we said. Later, planning for this trip to the Animal Kingdom where it is summer weather, the Gen'l says, "Mama, have you put in plenty of the iodine and carbolic oil?" "What are they for?" asks your Ma mildly. "For tick bites," says Gen'l S. "They bore under your skin to lay their eggs and you have to put on the oil to make them come out." "Suppose they don't come out?" says Ma. "Oh, well, then you get tick fever—but you always get them out. In the old days they dug them out with a knife."

This must all sound as if they were pulling long ones to scare the tenderfeet. But it's not that at all. It never occurs to them that these phenomena are not all in the day's work for us at home. They think no more of them than we do of the imminence of gangsters at home.

FCL and TWL were still abroad when Franklin Roosevelt later that month steamed into Pulpit Harbor on the presidential yacht Potomac. *FDR's sons had preceded him, cruising in on a sailboat. They issued a friendly summons to members of the Lamont clan at Sky Farm to come down to the harbor and meet the President on his arrival. It was just as well the clan's laird and lady, no admirers of FDR, were away. When in New York, it was FCL's wont, per the noted Helen Hokinson cartoon, to assemble a group of friends to join her at the Trans Lux theatre to boo the President on screen.*

TSL to TWL
North Haven, July 23, 1936

The Roosevelt boys seemed gregarious and friendly. They came up to our house to borrow milk, gin and a tennis racquet. They broke the tennis racquet . . . The next morning the President was to arrive, and airplanes began swooping around Pulpit Harbor, cruisers and destroyers came steaming up, and boats filled with reporters and photographers. The North Haven band went down on the point and played. The Roosevelt boys had told Tommy (ed. TWL II) that he and his brothers could come out and shake hands with their father, so the Lamont children and the Cabot children[1] went out and did the honors. Ellie didn't go out because she said she was afraid I would disapprove or that you would disapprove.

TWL to AL
Yeamans Hall, Charleston, S.C., December 1936

It has rained here a lot but we have worked in a surprising amount of golf and rest. The low-brow life for us! Walter L. (ed. Lippmann) has been reading aloud the last Agatha Christie, and Ma & I each won 75¢ in a hat pool guess as to the murderer. The table talk is all Mrs. Simpson and the King. I guess likely he ought not to marry her, but I think Baldwin[2] pulled a boner in pressing the issue to an immediate decision. Why not let the thing simmer for six months? A lot can happen in that time.

---

[1]The Boston Cabots lived across Pulpit Harbor from the Lamonts. Clustered together at the end of a point in a hodge-podge of rustic, weathered cottages, they viewed the showier New Yorkers of Sky Farm with a certain wariness. The Cabots may have spoken only to God (as the saying went), but FCL thought them not godly enough for her taste. They were known to play poker on Sunday.

[2]Prime Minister Stanley Baldwin.

Before leaving New York I went to an amusing dinner for all the leading actors and actresses in N.Y. I sat betwixt Cornelia Otis Skinner and Margelot Gilman. It seemed to me she (ed. COS) made a little effort to talk high sex stuff to me, very sober and dignified. "Don't you think, Mr. Lamont, that any woman, if she really and truly loves a man, if she really loves him from her heart, can win the love of that man? I think so, Mr. Lamont, indeed I do, with all my heart." It was all very crowded and intimate, rubbing elbows, etc. Miss Skinner deftly removed a pat of butter which a waiter had dropped on my shoulder. I suppose the waiter thought that the poor bankers had not been buttered up much lately and he would have a try...

Europe was tensing in 1937 as the Continent edged ever closer to armed conflict. Hitler's Germany was rearming with a vengeance. Il Duce, fresh from his conquest of Ethiopia, was strutting up a belligerent furor in Italy. Both he and Hitler had forged a devil's pact to aid Franco and his fascists in the civil war raging in Spain. None of this dissuaded TWL and FCL from making their annual sojourn abroad. As usual, they had more elevated things in mind.

FCL to TSL
Villa Aurelia, Porta San Pancrazio, Rome, April 1937

The other morning I got up early and went with Chester[1] and H. James[2] to the Sistine Chapel. Chester had gotten permission to take us up on the scaffolding where they are repairing the Michelangelo frescoes. We lay flat on our backs on the rough boards and I expected every minute to be hurled onto the pavement fifty feet below, as the scaffolding swayed and rocked every time anyone moved. But it was

[1] Chester Aldrich, director of the American Academy in Rome.
[2] Henry James, nephew of the novelist Henry James and son of the philosopher William James who had been one of TWL's professors at Harvard.

CL at Loch Lomond

wonderful to have that intimacy with those great paintings. I shall always feel as if Noah and Isaiah and the Delphic Sibyl were my intimate friends.

By July, the Lamonts and numerous offspring were ensconced in a rented manor in the Scottish highlands. There they spent the rest of the summer. The manor came fully staffed and overlooked Loch Lomond. Despite the glorious view, which reminded the Lamonts of their proud ancestral ties to the region, the experience drew a loud raspberry from FCL.

FCL to TSL
Ross Dhu, Luss, Dumbartonshire, August 1937

Never again, a whole summer away for us. We all hate it here. It rains every minute . . . Pa came home from his outing full of beans, but I came home with a temperature of 102° and was greeted with the news that the cook had been drunk the entire time I was away ("rollicking drunk" was the expression) and that the black donkey was in the kitchen all the time. It does seem too bad, with four cooks, that we have to have our meals cooked by a black donkey. The cook puts on an evening dress every night, heaven knows why.

Things were no better when TWL and FCL sojourned seven months later in a chateau on the French Riviera.

TWL to ELC
Eze, France, March 13, 1938

Metcalfe sounded the keynote for this place when he remarked sadly, "I hope to God I see New York again, but I don't expect it." The dumbwaiter, which was the special occasion for this adjuration, is the least of our ills. It is like an elevator running up through three stories, with the well wide open at each story, no enclosure whatsoever. An unwary footstep will send you hurtling down into the subterranean caves of this 11th-century abode.

The water pipes. Don't take a warm bath as the normal thing but as a gift from God. The electric lighting is made up of shreds and patches, no insulation of any kind, cords strung about here and there, with little tag ends of wire hanging out, and of course people tripping constantly over loose floor wires and putting everything on the blink. After 9 p.m. we are lost in darkness for the night—all except the bedroom closets where, for some curious reason, the system works. You get installed in bed, with a nice detective story, only to have your light expire with a gasp for the night, but still able to go to your clothes' press (in the closet) and witness your trousers hanging in brilliant illumination.

The bathrooms. If one has any serious writing or reading to be done, that is the place to do it. There are no locks or bolts that catch on the inside of the bathroom doors, but that is really immaterial, for the crevices are so enormous that the slightest noise from the bathroom goes all over the house. Brushing one's teeth sounds, out in the hall, like a buzzsaw. Every house over a thousand years old, as parts of this are, is bound to cherish the vestiges of both worse and better days. My bedroom and creaking bedstead preserve them in the form of fleas. I disrobe in a white enamel tub, but the little creatures elude me. Flit and Keating's Insect Powder are used by the gallon, but I'm still pretty blotchy.

The noise. We were not told beforehand that the village street runs through a section of the chateau right under your mother's bedroom. The village children and tourists make a great to-do at times right under us. The gardener produced a large sign—"Propriété Privée Chien Dangereux"—which he proposes to hang up so as to divert the traffic into another street. But that seems unfair unless we can truly boast of a dangerous dog. (The lights are flickering . . . not sure I can finish this.)

The golf course is perched on the serrated top of a 3,000-foot-high mountain. You pull your ball, it strikes a crag and goes hurtling out into space a thousand feet below. The stances you get are never on the same level with the ball—either far above it or way below it. Put a golf ball on the mantel shelf above you and practice a couple of approach shots, you'll get the idea. A good part of the time the entire links is shrouded in impenetrable fog. The play is helped along by the sudden shouts of caddies warning their players of some shot hurtling our way. The whole scheme is designed to develop the powers of concentration.

The cook and butler were, however, our worst trial. She had never cooked. He had never served. We stood it for two days, thinking we were just in a bad dream and would wake up. But the nightmare deepened. We finally got rid of them by paying them two-thirds of a month's salary. We now have a swell cook, a cordon bleu, and are likely to eat ourselves into a bilious attack. (Excuse me, Metcalfe just reports that all lights in the kitchen and pantry are out—and only a half-hour to dinner).

I wouldn't for words have our friends get the idea we were not happy here. It's just the rub of the green. and the new cook is a treasure. The sun is coming out tomorrow, the plum blossoms are in bloom, the hill towns are lovely, and your mother is already ordering clothes from the Cannes branch of Chanel's. So you see, the world is bright!

Much love
Da

Not so bright actually. That very day in '38 when TWL had written his daughter, Hitler's troops had marched into Austria. In a postscript to ELC, TWL wondered with prophetic irony whether Hitler's move to annex German's tiny neighbor wasn't "quite the limit." Closer to home, an unexpected personal scandal had brushed TWL and his colleagues at the bank. Richard Whitney, a former president of the New York Stock Exchange and brother of TWL's close friend and Morgan partner

George Whitney, had been arrested earlier that March in New York for embezzlement. TWL, at George's urgent request, had made an indirect loan to help Richard out of his jam before his arrest and subsequent sentencing to prison. TWL's unflinching loyalty took its toll on him.

FCL to TSL
Eze, France, March 1938

I was sorry to be so uncooperative on the telephone, but I was (& am) troubled about Father. He has not been well . . . . When all this Whitney thing came up, he was greatly troubled about it, and after those long telephone calls every night (ed. from TSL with the latest news on the scandal) he could not sleep and his heart began to "thump" (he calls it) and make a singing in his ears. We thought a day or two of rest would cure it, but his heart continues to throb and he is quite miserable. He thinks it was playing golf on a hilly course, but I think it is mostly just strain and worry. It is most unfortunate that he should be called home now. My point is that although it would be much better for the prestige of the Morgan firm to have him home now, it would be much worse for the firm to have him die and *never* be there. I think some way it will have to be managed for him to have a long rest to get his heart all quiet again. You must get more people in the firm and quickly . . .

Not content with pressuring her oldest son to get the bank to beef up its executive ranks, FCL let her second son know, in no uncertain terms, how she felt about Stalin and Russia.

FCL to CL
Eze, France, March 1938

I am wondering if all this Russian business is going to make any difference in our plans. (This *is* the rottenest pen.) To me, now that it is all over, it seems as if Stalin had been on trial, not the men. Take a man like Yagoda[1], a cruel filthy beast and a traitor—who put him in power? Stalin must have known the kind of cruel beast he was. But it suited Stalin's purposes to have a man like that who would ruthlessly 'liquidate' the people unpleasing to Stalin. Yes, Stalin knew the kind of man he was putting in power over all the helpless victims, a man without mercy or justice. Well, that's what you get in a tyranny like Russia. But why and how you can stand up for it beats me. You of all people on earth, you who even felt for the Harvard scrubwomen[2], who have always been for the underdog. Can't you realize that the end does not justify the means? That way lies dishonour and cruelty and lying. But it is as if your eyes were sealed. I pray every day that God will open your eyes to see the truth. Even if one believes in collective ownership, one does not have to believe in wading through blood and tears to get it.

FCL to AL and NL
Hyde Park Hotel, London, April 1938

We were three days in Paris, and then came here. The train ride from Folkestone was so lovely I almost wept. The meadows were unbelievably soft and green, the fruit trees all out, the banks studded with pale primroses, and the little lambs playing with their mothers, and bright sunshine over all. It was so peaceful, so restful, it was like a smile of God.

London is a whirl. We got here Friday and went down to Cliveden Saturday. Lady Astor had a huge dinner for Lord Halifax, the Duke of Kent, the Archbishop of Canterbury, five ambassadors all done up in ribbons and orders, and everyone you have ever heard of in Eng-

---

[1]The Soviet "show trials" had finally run their course. Hundreds of victims of Stalin's mass purge of dissidents and political opponents had been sentenced to execution or to Siberian labor camps. Yagoda, unidentified, was likely one of the key State prosecutors.

[2]CL at college had championed the cause of Harvard's underpaid maids and scrubwomen.

lish political or social life. It was just like a grand movie of the Passing Show. I sat at dinner between Walter Elliott & Sir John Simon[1].

Today we went to the Italian Embassy for luncheon. I did not want to go, but Papa carried on so & got so excited that I overcame my scruples. If Grandi[2] knew what I thought of his government he would have put poison in my egg. I sat next to the Danish ambassador and had a dull time.

FCL to CL
Cliveden, Taplow, April 2, 1938

It is a quiet weekend here, but no end of talk about Germany and Austria and Spain, etc. I hold my own fairly well. I do not think their views about Hitler are unreasonable[3]. I think everything should be done & tried to prevent a big war. The whole thing is so depressing. I do not see how we live at all. It is like some horrid nightmare. I keep thinking I shall wake up and find it isn't true. But with three madmen in Europe, what is going to be the outcome? Everything I heard about the things being done in Spain and Austria makes me crazy with impotent rage[4]. This beautiful world, and what have we done with God's gift?

TWL to CL
Blickling Hall, Aylsham, April 10, 1938

Welcome to the shores of Europe! I do hope your Russian trip will be all that you anticipated. But you can never tell what any of the

---

[1]John Simon, Britain's Chancellor of the Exchequer.

[2]Dino Grandi, Italy's Ambassador to London and former Foreign Secretary.

[3]Despite later charges that the influential Cliveden set favored appeasement of Hitler, FCL was in good company at the time. Although the Clivedenites despised Hitler, their conciliatory stance was shared by the government of the day and most Britons.

[4]Hitler's Brown Shirts were crushing all resistance in Austria to the Nazi-imposed Anschluss. In the Spanish civil war both sides were committing wholesale atrocities. Of particular note in the U.S., Franco's nationalist forces had decimated the American contingent fighting with the republicans' Lincoln-Washington Brigade.

totalitarian states will suddenly do. The interest of none would be served by war. All would go down in the funeral welter.

FCL to CL
Pinbury Park, Cirencester, April 1938

Here in England I have seen only people in favor of Chamberlain[1]. I long to hear the other side and next week I shall see Gilberto (ed. Gilbert Murray) and Lord Cecil and perhaps P. Noel-Baker[2].

I am almost convinced that the Perth-Ciano negotiations[3] were necessary and wise, but at the same time they made me sick. Perhaps there are times, politically as well as physically, when in consequence of not having done right, you have to take an emetic. I do hope the little states of the League won't vote to recognize Italy in Abyssinia.

What a glorious fight the Chinese are putting up[4]. I have seen something of the Chinese Ambassador, three times in fact. I won him over completely by telling him I had gone on a consumer's boycott of Japanese goods. I was at the Chinese Embassy when word was cabled in that there had been a smashing victory and 20,000 Japs had been killed. A great wave of delight and enthusiasm swept over the guests, in which I shared. Then I thought, "How horrible to rejoice that 20,000 of my fellow human beings have died in pain and terror." That is what war brings us to.

Yesterday, Easter Sunday, I went to the village church with Judith[5]. They read the passage, "He that dwelleth in love, dwelleth in God, and God in him, for God is love." Then soon the prayer came for peace on this earth and goodwill among men. It came over me, these

---

[1]Neville Chamberlain had succeeded Baldwin as Prime Minister.

[2]Philip Noel-Baker, British statesman and author.

[3]The negotiations by Galeazzo Ciano, Italy's foreign minister and Mussolini's son-in-law, and Sir James Perth, the British Ambassador to Rome, led to a short-lived Anglo-Italian pact of convenience which effectively condoned Mussolini's aggressions in Ethiopia and Spain. Chamberlain's opponents, led by Churchill, were outraged.

[4]The Sino-Japanese war had begun the previous year with Japan's invasion of northern China.

[5]Judith Masefield, daughter of John and Constance.

people praying here for peace, this nationwide prayer for peace and that love may be manifested, these are the really strong people. The nations that pray for love are the really strong nations. They are in tune with what is deepest in the nature of things, with unseen forces, and they cannot fail. "Not by might, nor by power, but by my spirit, saith the Lord of Hosts."

I rejoice that America is a Christian nation, too, and prays for love among men. Russia prays for class warfare, preaches hate among men. Hitler and Mussolini preach hate among nations. Thank God, there are people who believe in the victory of persuasion over force. If only I were younger to work harder for it. It is going to conquer, I know that. Forgive my Easter sermon.

FCL to CL
New York City, May 1938

The situation here goes from bad to worse. I never was in such a place of deep depression and discouragement. I felt it like a cloud the minute I walked off the gangplank. Father and Tommy both looked white and worried, and so does everybody else. The wicked thing about it is that it need not be. America is rich in resources and very hard-working, and this depression need not have been. Four months ago, Franklin (ed. FDR) could have stopped it. Now it is almost too late. I do think he is a very wrong-minded man, so intent on his own power & glory that he cannot think of the welfare of his country—just everything for Self. That is what happens to a world without religion. Oh for a big, generous, honest man with principles and intelligence. We do not seem to breed them anymore, in this country or in any other. Certainly not in the country you are interested in . . .

TWL to CL
New York City, May 25, 1938

We have had your bulletins of progress and were happy to hear your genial voice over the radio a week ago speaking from Moscow. Terribly sorry to know that the beer is flat over there . . .

FCL to CL and ML
New York City, June 1938

I have been reading an interview of yours, Corliss, in the *Daily Worker,* saying how absolutely perfect Russia is. If only you could stay there long enough to get at the truth . . .

TWL to CL
New York City, October 24, 1938

You were speaking the other day about the possibility of your issuing a statement to the general effect of denying that you were a Communist. It is certainly a puzzling situation and I sympathize with your perplexities. Looking at it purely objectively, did it not occur to you that the general public is bound to classify you roughly as a Communist just as long as you continue to stand up publicly, and sometimes perhaps almost passionately, for the Russian scheme of things?

CL to TWL
New York City, November 16, 1938

Thanks very much for your memorandum on the tendency of the public to consider me a Communist because of my sympathy for Soviet Russia . . . I think you are probably right that my writings and lectures on the Soviet Union are the chief element in creating this wrong impression. However, in America today the term Communist is flung around very loosely and used to smear all sorts of liberal and labor people who have never had any association with Russia at all. I suppose that in politics we must consider name-calling a more or less ineradicable phenomenon. In any case, I feel I must continue to say exactly what I think about various subjects, including the Soviet Union, no matter what the reaction and misunderstanding among certain purblind groups.

TWL to CL
The Mid-Ocean Club, Bermuda, March 7, 1939

Thank you for your note of February 14th enclosing your Valentine in the shape of "The Story of Soviet Progress". I cannot help asking myself whether in painting such a glowing picture, but at the same time almost covering over the sombre colors, you have not fallen far short in making a convincing impression. You will say that you have not hesitated to allude to the bad features. No, it is true, you have not. But you have done it with such loving solicitude for the erring child that he is made to appear rather a darling, even if at times he indulges in his little lapses.

As the portents of all-out war in Europe intensified, America's isolationists dug in. Charles Lindbergh became their most public spokesman. The hero of 1927 was now the avatar of something called the America First movement. Lindbergh was outspoken in his opposition to U.S. aid for Britain and to those "powerful elements" who seemed bent on involving America in the coming hostilities. His sentiments were an affront to TWL and FCL, devoted Anglophiles, causing a painful rift between the Lamonts and Lindbergh whose wife, the writer Anne Morrow Lindbergh, was the daughter of FCL's close friend Betty Morrow. That September the isolationists and their supporters staged an Anti-War Mobilization protest in Washington.

TWL to ELC
New York City, September 21, 1939

Your mother mentioned to me your commendation of Charles Lindbergh's broadcast. I thought it was dreadful. Not because we are all not just as anxious to keep America out of the war, but because the tendency of the broadcast was to harden public sentiment in the U.S.A. and line it up for the isolationists. There is no argument on the question of shall we go into the war, only what is the best way to keep out of the war. Having studied these matters at close range for a period far longer than Charles Lindbergh's entire lifetime, I among many others am convinced that there is no certainty of our being able to avoid war. But the greatest tangible hope lies in our making

CL with the Masefields in England, ca. 1938

it possible immediately for the Allies to get as much here in the way of material supplies as they care to buy and pay cash for. If they were able to do this, they would then indeed be fighting a battle for us and would stand a much better chance of holding off the Germans from themselves and, eventually, from ourselves as well.

You are a woman of such intelligence, and I have such respect for that intelligence, that I wish you would read some of the material on this matter. Don't let all this isolationist talk fool you. Charles Lindbergh ought to be the last person to think that we can stay wrapped up in cotton wool over here, because he was the first flyer from the West to span the Atlantic alone in less than thirty-six hours. We can do a lot of things, but we cannot isolate or insulate ourselves. The very best thing we can do to keep out of the war is to permit all the belligerents—even though Britain and France may happily be the chief ones to avail of it—to buy what they like from us and take it away to help equip themselves to fight against the domination of the world by those two gangsters, Hitler and Stalin.

Early on, TWL had evinced some naivete on the chances of war in Europe. Ever the optimist, he had continuously downplayed the portents. But when war finally came in early September 1939, he and FCL had advocated immediate aid to Britain. Their falling-out with the Lindberghs was a harbinger of their envelopment, all too soon, in family, social and political squabbles relating to Britain and Russia, two nations that would become key allies against the Axis powers as the conflagration spread across Europe.

TWL to CL
New York City, January 23, 1940

From time to time you have shown puzzlement and even indignation that the American public fails to understand and discriminate between a professing Socialist (even though not a party member), who upholds the ideals of Soviet Russia, and an actual Communist. To me it is not surprising that the public should make no discrimination between the two. Russia is the great Communist state: ergo, as their minds go, every American who upholds its ideals must be pro-Communism. And it is no distance at all from being pro-Communist to being Communist itself.

FCL to CL
North Haven, July, 1940

Your letter filled me with a sort of terror. Either you are (1) a slight mental case, or else (2) intoxicated when you wrote, or else (3) through your loyalty to Russia, so blinded to the truth that you can no longer see things or hear things as they are. This distresses me.

At my birthday party, no one advocated that Britain should make peace, and no one even hinted that Hitler should be persuaded to attack Russia. Everyone said that it would be fine if America could have better relations with Russia, but asked the question "How?" Fortunately, Austin is here. I consider him a reliable witness. A scientific training makes one give weight to facts. He agrees with me that you are wrong in your statements contained in the letter. Really, Corliss, nobody hinted that Hitler should attack Russia (although I suppose most Americans would prefer it to having him attack England). Charlie Merz[1] asked a purely hypothetical question about what *could* be honourable peace terms. But no one thought it possible.

Really, you *must* stick to facts, you must listen and not distort what people say. You are so down on England and so down on capitalists that you do not give us a fair chance. Honestly, this worries me terribly. The essence of fair play is to be fair & just to those with whom you disagree.

[1]Charles Merz, Editor of the New York *Times*.

FCL to CL
North Haven, Summer 1940

Have you read recent editorials about Russia in the *Times* and *Tribune*? Or do you only read editorials favourable to Stalin, like only going to see plays that do not criticize totalitarian states? (This isn't any more a dig at you than your telling me I get all my news from dinner-party gossip).

I have continued to work for ships for children[1], and have made a perfect pest of myself. People hate to see me coming. Also I feel very passionately about letting the British have 60 of our destroyers. How cruelly America is going to pay for her blindness, ignorance & callousness. The trouble is my generation will be dead and gone, and all the Nyes & Vandenburgs, Clarks & Wheelers[2], etc. (I'd like to burn them all in boiling oil) will be dead and gone, and no one left but the generation of my beloved grandchildren and perhaps children. I know we have got to have conscription—but, Lord, how I hate it. *How I hate it.* That is what the people who will not help England have brought us to.

Tommy has two of his refugee children here, English, aged 11 and 9[3]. They came to church in queer little dresses & large white sunbonnets, and all the congregation were agog.

P.S. What did you think of Lindbergh's last speech? If he comes here again, Austin has promised me to take him sailing and drown him.

---

[1]FCL, like many Americans, was concerned with the fate of thousands of British children who might be trapped with their families in the event of a successful Nazi invasion of Britain. Many families in the U.S., including TSL's, had opened their homes to young refugees from England. FCL, however, was unhappy that the U.S. government would not send ships across the Atlantic to save the children from, in her words, "death and starvation."

[2]FCL refers to a quartet of Senate Republican leaders known for their rock-ribbed conservatism and opposition to involving America in the European conflict.

[3]Two daughters of Francis Rodd, a.k.a Lord Rennell of Rodd. While the father was serving in Britain's wartime intelligence forces, Lady Rodd and her children moved into the TSL's weekend house on Long Island, New York.

That summer of '40, TWL announced his support for the Republican presidential candidacy of Wendell Willkie. Indeed, TWL had been instrumental in the financing and stage-managing of Willkie's nomination. Willkie was not only a driving business executive in the Morgan internationalist mold, he favored unqualified support for Great Britain. He badly lost the election that fall to Roosevelt. TWL offered his condolences to Willkie, his congratulations to FDR, then reverted to the more comfortable paterfamilias role.

TWL to CL
New York City, December 19, 1940

I promised myself I would comment on your letter of December 6th regarding Russia.

I don't at all hold with all this chatter of yours about "propaganda" and "people's unworthy motives" and all that sort of thing. We are all just about alike. Mr. Hull[1], for example, is as fine a man as anyone I have ever met in public or private life. If you were running a government, you would find it was necessary to have political considerations in mind to a certain extent even if they were not the guiding ones . . .

Finally, when you speak of "the hypocrites, knaves and fools . . . in the English-speaking countries" am I to understand that none of these categories are to be found in Russia? No, my dear fellow, you get nowhere by calling people names. There are very few wise men, but, aside from the dictators, there are fewer knaves than you seem to imagine. Seriously, one can never become a leader of men if one takes the attitude that he is surely right and the other fellow wrong.

[1]Secretary of State Cordell Hull.

TWL to AL
New York City, February 4, 1941

. . . Sometime, Austin, around 8:30 p.m. don't you want to call up your Uncle Jack at Winter Park and have a little chat with him? I know he would be so grateful. He is terribly lonely. I try to call him up every week and sometimes twice a week, and he just longs for the sound of a family voice. Nothing in particular, just to show him that you are thinking of him in his loneliness.

TWL to CL
Yeamans Hall, South Carolina, March 9, 1941

I think I like this much better than Florida. It is more bracing, and the urge of cocktail parties is less. Your Ma has, however (and this is a gain), managed to become quite fond of a Dubonnet cocktail. Her excuse is: "I think what I like about it is the quinine in it." Sic!

TWL to CL
North Haven, August 1941

Dear Cor—Had ¾ hour with FDR and Harry Hopkins on the *Potomac* when it came into Pulpit Harbor last Friday for the night. H.H. most interesting about Russia & Stalin. Better come up soon and let me tell you all about it.

On August 15 FDR paid a return visit to Pulpit Harbor, this time with his close advisor Harry Hopkins in tow. They had just returned from a secret meeting with Churchill in Newfoundland where the two leaders had blocked out a declaration in principle of the Allies' postwar aims, later known as the Atlantic Charter. Earlier, Hopkins had flown to Moscow to meet with Stalin and assess the Russians' needs following Hitler's invasion of the U.S.S.R. that June. TWL had invited himself aboard the Potomac. *He was thrilled at FDR's description of the meeting with Churchill, fascinated by Hopkins's glowing appraisal of Stalin. FDR's and Hopkins' doubts about the Japanese, the chance of war erupting in the Far East, seemed not to have fazed TWL. He was still professing unconcern about the Far East three weeks before the Japanese bombed Pearl Harbor on December 7th.*

FCL to AL at Wisconsin General Hospital, Madison, Wis.
New York City, December 22, 1941

A happy Christmas to you—how we shall miss you. It will not be the same without you at all. In fact, I really fear it is going to be a poor Christmas, with this horrible war hanging over us. Aunt Anne sent me a Christmas card with an old carol printed on it,

"Joseph did whistle
And Mary did sing
And all the bells
On earth did ring
For joy the Lord was born."

I am going to try to be like Joseph and Mary, and whistle and sing.

One by one, FCL's and TWL's sons would be drawn to the war. TSL would leave the bank to join the Army's Eighth Air Force, assigned to London as a procurement officer foraging for scarce parts and supplies for American bombers. CL embarked on a coast-to-coast tour to solicit public support for America's beleaguered ally Russia. AL was relocated to the Midwest on temporary training duty with the Army's Medical Reserve Corps. ELC's husband, Charles Cunningham, joined the Navy. Too soon, so would FCL's and TWL's first grandson and namesake, Thomas W. Lamont II.

TSL at Palisades in late 1930s

FCL to AL
Torrey Cliff, Palisades, December 26, 1941

Christmas Day was warm and bright. The children were eager and appreciative of all their presents and one and all behaved remarkably well. We had the usual Christmas tree celebration, all sitting in the hall and singing carols while we waited for Santa.

I heard Winston Churchill today addressing Congress. I thought it quite an historic event, and his speech was superb.

I did not agree with Nancy about your taking a slightly more comfortable room (ed. at AL's training station), and neither did Pa. You are 36 and cannot do just like a young intern. The job is the thing, and if you could do a high-class job, a better job, by living on nightingales' tongues, I should make an effort to get them. I think it is really necessary for you to use your strength getting ahead in your work and not dissipate it with sleepless nights. You are not spoiled, and I won't have you say so. It is a reflection on me! If you were in the Army in Africa and couldn't sleep well, you would be given strength to stand it with the best of them. But as long as you *don't* have to stand it, it would be silly.

A blessed calm has descended on the house as the children eat their supper. They are entranced with the revolving Christmas tree that plays "Silent Night" as it goes around. Do you remember it?

We missed you terribly yesterday. I am sure you missed all of us, too.

FCL to CL in California
New York City, January 1942

We all sent you blessings & thoughts on New Year's Day and missed you no end. I wonder if you saw the *Times* editorial for January 1st called "Yes—A Happy New Year". It was excellent. I am so sick & tired of these sour-pusses who can't even wish you a "Merry Christmas".

I have been attacked savagely because of my well known sympathies with Russia on account of the article that appeared in *Pravda.* I do wish it had not been written. When all of us are trying to create a nice feeling for & appreciation of Russia, this article undoes months of work. People are resentful of it. I think it is bad. I called up Margaret (ed. Corliss' wife) and she said the Russians were just playful when they compared America to a ladybug lying on its back waving its feet in the air. Too bad they didn't check that playful impulse. If they want American help (and they do), they must not call us cowardly. It is an ugly word.

This letter is just to bring you love and let you know I am thinking of you. I can't decide whether you are in more danger from bombs or from those dizzy Hollywood blondes. Go easy, my dear boy.

The war had not yet dented FCL's style of living or penchant for literary salons in her Manhattan townhouse.

FCL to AL
New York City, January 1942

The weeks since Christmas have been extremely busy.

Julian Huxley is living here now, rather indefinitely, but I enjoy having him and he makes no trouble at all for anyone. There was a rushy time when Edna St. Vincent Millay[1] and her big bushy husband were here, and the Charles Morgans[2] at the same time, also Julian. Mrs. Morgan and Edna St. V. immediately went to bed, both of them. They had different doctors, and there was a period of croup kettles, gargles, etc., with all meals carried on trays to husbands and wives alike.

Edna is going to do some work for the Red Cross. I felt my taking her in was part of my contribution to the Red Cross. She is a dear person, but she is drinking herself to death. It is terribly sad. She drinks so much that she doesn't care for eating and would come up for a delicious dinner, then eat a piece of parsley and half a roll. I had one nice evening with her when all the men went out, and she read her poetry out loud to me.

Corliss seems to be having a triumphant tour of the Pacific Coast. I believe he is doing worthwhile work, as I regard it of the utmost importance that we should help Russia, and I find prejudice (ed. against Russia) rampant on every side, even here in the East. Charlie C. has applied for a job in some Navy department. Eleanor says it could take him to Dakar or anywhere.

We are having a grand dinner party for Julian on the 23rd. Ambassador Steinhardt[3] is coming, Wendell Willkie, the Robert

---

[1] Edna St. Vincent Millay, the celebrated American poet and Bohemian.

[2] Charles Morgan, novelist and drama critic for the *Times* of London; his wife Hilda Vaughan was the author of numerous books.

[3] Laurence Steinhardt, U.S. Ambassador to Russia.

Moseses[1], the Reids[2], the Anne O'Hare McCormicks[3]. Did you ever know such a galaxy of stars? I did not mean it to be so. Robert Frost[4] comes for a night or two on the 20th on his way south. *That* I do look forward to.

FCL to AL
New York City, January 31, 1942

It has been an exciting ten days since I last wrote you . . .

Ambassador Litvinoff and his wife came to tea[5]. He is an intelligent old fox and seems to have nice moral ideas of international relations. I suppose, though, he would just as soon slit our throats as look at us. Pa says I must not mention the fact of the Litvinovs being here.

Another absorbing evening was at a dinner with Dorothy Thompson[6]. She talked every single minute in a loud shrill voice, but I thought her well worth listening to . . . Robert Frost was here for two days—a great refreshment for the spirit. He has one of the two or three really original minds I have ever met. Most conversation is like this letter. You tell A what B said, or what you read in a book that C wrote. But Robert Frost gets it all out of himself, and it is good and fresh and unhackneyed.

Julian is still here. He is practically no trouble materially, but he sometimes is a bother socially. He always wants to do a good part of the talking no matter if you are dying to hear what Frost or someone is saying. He is extremely bright, but not a really first-class mind . . . Lord Halifax[7] was here for breakfast today. He has a good mind and a wonderful character, but is so lacking in fire. What can we do about it? Vitamins?

---

[1]Robert Moses, New York's master planner, road builder and power broker.

[2]Ogden and Helen Rogers Reid, owners of the New York *Herald Tribune.*

[3]Anne O'Hare McCormick, the distinguished New York *Times* foreign affairs columnist.

[4]Robert Frost, the poet.

[5]Maxim Litvinov, Soviet Ambassador to the United States.

[6]Dorothy Thompson, the widely syndicated *Herald Tribune* columnist.

[7]Lord Halifax, now the British Ambassador to Washington.

I hope to go up to Boston next week for a few days. Eleanor seems very blue over Charlie's going. I should think she would be.

FCL to AL
New York City, February 11, 1942

I want to tell you about the Red Cross service at St. Thomas's Church a week ago where Father read the lesson, the Beatitudes[1].

Raymond Massey, the actor, gave the address. The church is moving when a high church episcopal lets an actor go into the pulpit and preach the sermon[2]. Father read the Beatitudes beautifully. The West Point choir sang, 150 cadets. They marched up the aisle, in uniform, followed by Red Cross nurses in uniform. You knew that they were all probably going to the front soon, and it made you want to cry. They looked so earnest and young. The church was filled with mothers and sweethearts of the boys & girls. The whole thing was very moving. It swept over me in a wave of conviction that the only thing that could possibly comfort these people was some kind of religious faith, a belief that this great experiment of life and consciousness in the universe had a deep meaning and was rooted in a spiritual force. It is the only thing that seems to make sense. Otherwise, it seems like a tale told by an idiot, full of sound and fury and signifying nothing.

Charles goes Monday to Newport for training in Naval Intelligence.

TWL to AL
Yeamans Hall, S.C., February 22, 1942

Last Wednesday, Tommy went up into the Laurentians skiing with Stuart Craigin and another officer of our bank. Tommy missed Stu-

---

[1]TWL had been appointed chairman of the Red Cross National Advisory Committee as part of a major fund-raising campaign for the organization.

[2]Raymond Massey was not only an accomplished actor but a member of one of Canada's most prominent families, leaders in the fields of diplomacy and religious and educational philanthropy.

TWL above the salt, 1941

art late the next afternoon, went out alone to find him, discovered him buried and helpless in a large snowdrift some miles away. Ribs broken, couldn't move, and would have frozen to death that night. Tommy succeeded in dragging him out, got help, and he was patched up. Next day Tommy's other friend landed on some rocks and broke his head. Tommy retrieved him and they took several stitches in his scalp. Tommy telegraphed Harry Davison (ed. another young Morgan partner) that he had given up skiing until he had finished being a St. Bernard . . .

That winter TWL busied himself in the war effort as a leading fund-raiser for the Red Cross and United China Relief. At the same time, he was reassuring friends abroad that the war would not separate America from them indefinitely. To an Italian colleague, he wrote, "Some time or other, dear Nino, a new day will dawn and America and Italy will once more be friends. But before that day comes there will be fire and flame and sword, grief for us all." FCL, with her two oldest sons immersed in war-related work, channeled her religiosity, her Anglophilia and her lusty FDR-phobia into letters to her youngest son now training for a career in anesthesiology.

FCL to AL
Yeamans Hall, February 27, 1942

I am getting a good rest—at least I would be, if I hadn't in a moment of insanity promised to talk for 15 minutes on the radio for the World Council of Churches. I am trying to write my speech and it is rotten, lousy, bum. It is so hard to say anything that is not a mere generality, and after all who is Florence Lamont that she should tell the church in America and England how they should behave in these war days? It is preposterous that I should do it. I spent a precious morning of sunshine writing the most awful balderdash. I am beginning to wish a German bomb would put an end to my sufferings.

Did you see Walter L's article last Tuesday, calling Roosevelt "the bottleneck of bottlenecks" and mentioning the fact of his "inertia and complacency"? I am sorry to say I enjoyed reading it more than I do my Bible . . .

FCL to AL
Yeamans Hall, March 6, 1942

. . . We continue to read out loud "Flight to Arras" by St. Exupery[1]. You must read it. You can't devote the whole 168 hours a week to anesthesia.

[1] Antoine de Saint-Exupery, the French aviator and author.

FCL to AL
New York City, April 6, 1942

I went to a Good Friday service and heard the moderator of the Church of Scotland, Dr. Cockburn, speak. It was a remarkable sermon—not one word about the war or democracy, and yet you went out feeling you must give all you had in you . . . What is there about a tip-top Englishman or Scotchman that is so superior? Their faces, their voices, their minds, their spirit? Of course, we have some similar ones here, but not nearly as many. I do not understand what the quality is—they have a quality of "distinction". Some of our best men are good and noble and bright, but not distinguished.

TWL to AL
New York City, April 20, 1942

Yesterday, as your mother may have written you, she and I went over to the Arthur Sulzbergers[1] in Westchester for luncheon to meet all the newspaper publishers from around the country. Everybody seemed to be there except the Smart Set, which was a good thing. Jesse Jones[2] and Eugene Meyer[3], who had the fisticuffs last week, were within six feet of each other, but nothing exploded. I brought Colonel McCormick of the Chicago *Tribune* over to our table for luncheon. Your mother hadn't met him before. She was appalled at his views.

David Bowes-Lyon, Queen Elizabeth's brother, was there, just in from England. He asked me whether I remembered when last we met, and I recalled it was Lord Lothian's place at Blickling in July 1939[4]. "You remember," he said, "while we were walking in the garden that lovely Sunday morning, what you said to me? You said, 'If war comes, America may never get into the fighting, but of one thing you can be sure—if Britain is up to her ears, America will furnish all the

[1]Arthur Sulzberger, publisher of the New York *Times.*
[2]Jesse Jones, U.S. Secretary of Commerce.
[3]Eugene Meyer, owner and publisher of the Washington *Post.*
[4]Lord Lothian, British statesman and Ambassador to the U.S. in 1939.

munitions and supplies that she needs, and there will be no talk of cash payments and governmental debts.' That statement," continued Bowes-Lyon, "was a great comfort to me and to all our family."

I gasped a bit. Gosh! People do take one so seriously. But it did come true in the Lend-Lease Bill[1].

FCL to AL
New York City, June 1942

I am just back from Exeter where I went for Tommy's graduation[2]. I am so glad I braced up and went. Tommy did remarkably well. His oration was well written, well thought out, and beautifully delivered. But I did not agree with a word of it. It was young Corliss speaking—all for the Socialist state and the New Deal, and anti-religious. But it was good . . . I had not been in Exeter since your graduation. Everything was the same. The beautiful old street, the magnificent elms—only *I* had changed. I felt a thousand years old.

FCL to AL
Torrey Cliff, June 19, 1942

Thank you for your interesting letter. I still do not understand what made you change your mind. The letter from Dr. Blalock, saying that they needed you at Johns Hopkins, seemed quite conclusive to me. If you go to the Army, you are one anaesthetist. If you can train a dozen men, you are twelve. I do not think, either, that you can decide as if you were absolutely free. You have four little children and can do for them what no one else on earth can do. The financial part is the least a good father does for his children. This is the reason that I am not happy about Tommy (ed. TSL) going into the Army and probably going way off. I think he ought to take one of the several important Washington jobs that have been offered him. For his three boys really need him.

[1]The Lend-Lease Act of 1941 authorized the transfer of war material to those nations in World War II whose defense was deemed vital to the security of the U.S.
[2]TWL II served as his class valedictorian.

TWL to ELC in Seattle
New York City, July 2, 1942

. . . Your brother Tommy received a commission (Major) in the U.S. Army on Monday, and they are talking seriously of sending him overseas in connection with large supply questions. Nothing has been decided, but my guess is that it would be across the Atlantic rather than any other direction. Your mother is not happy about it, but the rest of us, including Ellie, seem to think it is a fine assignment.

That summer TWL's and FCL's oldest son departed for wartime London. Their oldest grandchild, TWL II, was adamant about leaving Harvard to enlist in the Navy when he turned 18 in October. There were premonitions of tragedy and heartbreak ahead. A certain fatalism imbued the musings of FCL and her second son.

CL to FCL and TWL
New York City, Summer 1942

When Tommy was getting ready to leave for England, I wrote him a letter to say goodbye and tell him how much I appreciated the integrity and courage of his action. Among other things, I said something along these lines: that these were pretty tough times for the world and that during a terrific war, especially, one could never foretell what might happen to any individual; that that held for the various members of our own family; but that anyway we had all had a wonderful life together, and what else could you ask?

Sometimes here alone during the summer I have turned on the radio about 10 o'clock in the evening and listened to some light music and let my mind wander into the past. I find I have an infinite number of memories. Almost always I first return to Englewood and the big house on Beech Road, thinking of the football games and track meets that we used to hold on the field up toward the barn, of playing tennis on the sunken court now overgrown with grass, of playing kick-the-stick around the front porch, of coasting on the lawn toward Jones Road and of course down Mountain Road itself, of reading Andrew Lang's fairly tales in the library, of playing the old pianola and sitting after meals on the long back porch and hearing cows low in the field across the road.

Then there were the walks . . . to Pierce's Pond in the winter where I learned to skate. My old friend Berkie Reidemeister lived up that way, and I often ran home down the long hill, and one day in a rainstorm ran by a tree that a second later was struck by lightning which ripped the bark off it right down to the ground. Englewood has more happy memories for me that any other place where we've ever lived. But I also remember . . . the Swiss Alps in 1912; Easthampton and Mr. Mueller's Boys Club and Three Mile Harbor and the surf bathing and a pool table in our house; the two summers at "Flying D" Ranch and Klamath Lake, with the camping trips in the Spanish peaks and the Canadian Rockies, and wading down those streams in big rubber boats, fishing trout with Father . . . the summer in Idaho, going up to the wonderful Yellowstone at the end, although Glacier Park on one of our previous jaunts was even more beautiful.

I remember plain as day Northeast Harbor, climbing the mountains and picking blueberries, the courtship between Phil and Mrs. Savage[1] . . . Dark Harbor and learning to sail and the trip around 700-Acre Island in the fog . . . all those years at North Haven. Sailing anywhere else always seems dull in comparison with Penobscot Bay . . . Exeter and Harvard . . . Palisades . . . the noble mansion at 107 East 70th Street, with its procession of noble men . . . Geneva and Europe in 1924 . . . Oxford, London, and was it Naples in the spring of 1925? Uncle Jack and Aunt Lucy, the Masefields and H.G. Wells.

The point is, no children in all the world ever had a more varied, interesting, thrilling and happy life than you gave us all the years of our youth. Your great share in our work and joys and our own chil-

[1]Philip Savage, the Lamonts' longtime chauffeur.

Sky Farm, summer 1940s
Left to right (back row): TSL and wife Ellie; TWL and FCL; CL and wife Margaret; (kneeling) AL's wife Nancy, ELC.

dren continues as ever right up to the present. So whatever the future holds, none of us can be anything but grateful for practically the whole of the past. For my own part, I think I have had a darned good life, and if it ended tomorrow morning, I can't see that I would have much to kick about.

Your loving son

FCL to TSL in London
North Haven, July 1942

I have talked so much abut sending you 'protecting thoughts', etc., that I thought I should like to tell you what I really did think even at the risk of your thinking me rather silly & crazy.

I have just finished reading President Conant's address to the graduating class, in which he makes a very definite confession of his faith[1]. He says, "Experience seems to show that few men will fight fiercely against desperate odds unless they are imbued with a living faith; it would be my contention that for most of the American people today the final answers to the questions propounded by the facts of life and death must be in terms that no atheist would admit. For the vast majority of us the answers will involve the basic tenets of Christianity."

I believe that what is highest in man is deepest in the nature of things and I call this God, and have reason to believe that I can in some strange way get in touch with it. I believe it to be spiritual without any clear idea of what that means, something of the nature of mind, and that this something is the source and base of my being, without which I could not exist.

So with that as background, I have tried to write out the way I pray for you and think about you every day, hoping that it may be a protective thought for you in the days ahead with the chances for fine work, and also dangerous work perhaps.

Your devoted Mother

[1]James Bryant Conant, president of Harvard.

FCL to TSL
North Haven, August 6, 1942

I am exhausted because I have been scrubbing on my hands & knees. The adorable Nicky[1] came to my room with a beaming face and a basket of raspberries. Austin[2] inadvertently gave him a push. Down went the raspberries all over my new velvet rug, the juice running out in all directions. Then Nicky & Austin tried to pick up the berries, and ground them all nicely into the carpet . . . Papa is back from fishing. He brought a large box of trout. As they were caught several days ago, and have spent 17½ hours in trains, two nights in hotels, etc., I am dreading them. But Papa is so proud of them that I am going to eat them tonight, come what may. So this may be the last letter you will ever get from me.

TWL to TSL
North Haven, August 6, 1942

Ellie sent up this a.m. your letters 2 and 3. They are awfully interesting. I know it is not possible for you in a letter to describe your work. But from all the press accounts it is evident that the U.S.A. is getting more and more men over to the British Isles . . . Life here goes on just as it always does, except upon an immensely contracted basis. There are about ⅖ or ⅓ of the usual summer residents. The old life is gone . . .

FCL to CL
North Haven, August 1942

I read with great interest your article on *The Meaning of Humanism.* Oh, it comes so near the truth. It is pathetic that you can't quite get it. Humanism can never, never quite satisfy the human heart. You must know that in the depths of your being. There is nothing earth

[1]FCL's grandson Nicholas Lamont, the second son of AL.
[2]AL's first son and namesake.

can give us that will satisfy us. I have been reading a book about Henry Vaughan[1] that Aunt Bertha gave me. I am haunted by some verses he wrote about his brother's death:

"And yet as angels in some brighter dreams
Call to the soul when man doth sleep,
So some strange thoughts transcend our wanted themes,
And into glory peep."

Oh, that is what we all want—to get a glimpse, even a tiny one, even for the fraction of a second, of God's glory. We are so filled with fear & anxiety & grief.

Ellie & Nancy gave the tea at the Casino[2] yesterday, rather a meager one, as we could not spare any sugar for cake. (By the way, don't forget your sugar card if you come) . . . I was horribly depressed about Dieppe[3]. I could not sleep that night. Have we really got to wade through such a terrific bath of blood?

What do you think about Russia now? She is being incredibly brave, but will she hold? Don't think I do not want a second front[4] and that I do not know we have to lose many, many lives. But I felt Dieppe was so hopeless, nothing gained.

FCL to TSL
North Haven, August 1942

Life goes on here . . . We went to Hog Island. It has a marvelous beach where pure white pebbles grow. Do you remember it? Also lovely big meadows sloping down to the sea, with waving tawny

[1]Henry Vaughan, 17th-century English metaphysical poet who signed himself Silurist.
[2]The Casino was the North Haven yacht club house.
[3]Dieppe, the port city in Normandy, which on August 19, 1942 was the object of an attack by Allied commands to test German defenses. The attack force, largely Canadian troops, suffered terrible casualties.
[4]Plans for a second front in Europe, to relieve the defending Soviet armies on the Eastern Front, were being pushed by Stalin.

grass . . . I had a wonderful letter from General Smuts[1]. How that man, in the midst of commanding troops and planning strategy, can get time to sit down and write a longhand letter all about philosophy, as well as war, beats me. I felt braced and cheered by his letter.

FCL to TSL
North Haven, August 28, 1942

Tommy (ed. TWL II) came up last weekend with a girl, as I am sure Ellie must have written you. It made me feel a thousand years old to have a grandson who was beginning to be interested in girls. Tommy was just as amusing as he could be (not meaning to be), like Ken in *Mrs. Miniver*[2], very self-conscious and wanting the family to appear at their best. He referred to his little brother & sister & cousins as bad-mannered little brats and groaned horribly when I told him to be early for Sunday luncheon because the little children were coming. And it was just a minute ago he was one himself. He was so true to type as a 17-year-old. The little girl was very nice, English. Tommy took me into his confidence about various things, said he could always "reason" with me. I tried to give good advice.

A few days later a frightening episode dampened a family outing on Penobscot Bay.

TWL to ELC
New York City, September 10, 1942

Labor Day we planned a family picnic on Burnt Island. There were 21 of us altogether and we went in the 17-footer, the Fox Eye, plus

---

[1]Field Marshal Smuts had become a committed wartime ally and supporter of Great Britain.
[2]*Mrs. Miniver*, the very popular movie about a family under duress in Britain during the war, starring Greer Garson.

the blue Dinghy, and the *Posy L*[1]. There was a strong southwest wind blowing. After lunch, the wind had freshened. Tommy, Bill Rand (ed. a teenage family friend) and Lansing (ed. TWL II's 12-year-old brother) wanted to come home in the 17-footer. Austin said to Tommy, "All right, but be sure to take a reef in your mainsail before you start."

The rest of the family returned from the picnic on the Posy L, *towing the Dinghy, except for TWL II's mother, Ellie, who elected to sail the Fox Eye home.*

Ellie sailed a good careful course down along the island, keeping out of the worst of the wind. Tommy, on the other hand, failed to take a reef, headed out into the Bay, and we could see he was having a pretty wet time of it. He insisted upon sailing too close to the wind. Before we reached the Pulpit we could see that the 17-footer had tacked over behind Webster Head (ed. a wooded headland on the northeastern end of North Haven), presumably to get easier going. But she did not emerge before we turned the corner. Austin said he felt uneasy and thought he would go right back with the *Posy L.*

The next news was that, about half an hour after we reached home, Tommy called up from some house, half-drowned and breathless, to say that the 17-footer had sunk and he and the two others had had to swim for shore. They had gotten a life belt around Lansing so he was all right, but the other two had swum over 200 yards in a high sea and with all their clothes on.

It seems that they took in their own jib, but they were pretty badly filled with water. Tommy came in behind Webster Head to get straightened out. Then, about 200 or 300 yards from shore, Tommy

[1]The 17-footer, *El Jaleo,* was a small sloop of the Knockabout class; the Fox Eye was a 14-foot sailboat of Hereshoff design; the 12-foot blue Dinghy was one of the traditional North Haven Dinghies, the oldest known racing class in America; the *Posy L* was the family motor launch.

TWL and TWL II picknicking on Maine island, 1941

sent Bill forward to reset the jib, whereupon the water in the cabin rushed forward and the 17-footer sank by the Head like a stone. So they were in for it. Tommy began apologizing about the boat. I didn't give a darn about that. But I knew that Austin must be going through anguish, which he was. I directed Tommy to send out couriers to the beach to signal him, and started both Philip in the station wagon and Nancy in the Model T to go to the end of the island and do the same thing.

Austin had found the 17-footer with a foot of mast showing above the water and no sign of the boys, and he thought they were gone. There was a big set-up to the east (ed. a moving storm) and he followed the shore, wondering whether he could come across any traces. He just chanced to turn and luckily saw Nancy waving frantically. So it ended all right after a very bad scare. These young boys think they know all about sailing and may get a lesson too much at some time or other. You and Charlie know how strong the early September southwesters are—almost like a gale. It was an awfully narrow squeak.

The incident seemed in retrospect a premonition at worst, at the very least a sharp warning signal. TWL II displayed at times a daring, almost reckless attraction to high risk, in this case the dangerous sea. That fall, over his family's objections, he entered the Navy. A year later, having washed out as a Naval flier but still eager for action, he promptly signed on as a submariner in the so-called 'silent service'. His ship, the USS Snook, *bound for the Pacific, experienced at least one close call while test-diving on maneuvers.*

TWL to ELC
New York City, October 5, 1942

Young Tommy threw a bombshell into camp last week by saying that he had enlisted in Naval Aviation although he was just one day over eighteen. Enlistment, however, had to be subject to his parents' consent. He was already a member of the R.O.T.C.[1]. We all thought it very foolish. We could understand his wanting the excitement of this, that and the other, especially the atmosphere in which he is bound to work. But we all are agreed that for him, because his judgment is not very steady, it would be infinitely better for him to complete the R.O.T.C. two-year course at college and really be qualified to do something other than to make a poor flyer. Ellie thinks he would be a punk flyer, doubts whether he could even qualify because, to tell the truth, he doesn't even drive a car very well.

FCL to TSL in London
Torrey Cliff, Palisades, October 5, 1942

I want to tell you how fine and helpful Corliss has been about Tommy's latest wishes for enlisting in Naval Aviation. We all feel that, next to Ellie, it was owing to C that Tommy has given it up for the time being and will stay at Harvard in the R.O.T.C. We feel that C had more influence with Tommy than Grandpa had because, after all, one can always think one's grandfather is an ultraconservative.

Austin is starting in at Bellevue[2]. He is working hard and his decks are all stripped for action. Corliss is organizing a mass meeting of 20,000 in Madison Square Garden, for Russia . . . I think of you a great deal and pray for you and send you many good thoughts. Your letters sound as if you were feeling fairly well. Do you really get enough to eat? Egg powder sounds pretty grim to me.

That November, CL presided at a packed rally for Soviet-American friendship in Madison Square Garden. Vice President Henry Wallace spoke, as did TWL who, despite his denunciation of Communism,

[1] Reserve Officers' Training Corps.
[2] Bellevue Hospital, New York City.

praised Russia's "heroic stand" at Stalingrad, comparing it with the Greeks' defense of Thermopylae. It was the first and only time TWL shared a public platform with CL. FCL meanwhile immersed herself in Russian War Relief work.

TWL to ELC
New York City, December 15, 1942

There are not enough hours in the day, and all the hours are too short. Last week I spent two nights on the train going to Pittsburgh, inspecting the steel plants there. (ed. TWL was a director of the U.S. Steel Corporation). Then I spent Friday and Saturday in an economic conference at Princeton. Last Monday, Pearl Harbor Day, I had to speak on the steps of the sub-Treasury for the American Red Cross . . . John Cowles[1] has gone with Ed Stettinius[2] in Lend Lease. Without knowing anything about it, I have a notion they may both be moving over to North Africa before very long[3]. Tommy (ed. TSL) would have liked, I think, to be sent from London, but it wasn't so arranged. Ted Curtis[4] of Rochester went as General Spaatz's aide[5].

Of course, we were all dismayed by the terrible Cocoanut Grove catastrophe and only thankful that none of our own people were there. I think it was a close shave at that[6]. Here is an interview in *The Exonian* with an Exeter boy who was on the spot and helped—one of Francis Plimpton's boys[7] .

---

[1]John Cowles was the Minneapolis newspaper publisher and TWL's cousin.
[2]Edward R. Stettinius Jr. was Lend-Lease administrator, 1941-43.
[3]The North Africa campaign had reached a critical phase for the Allied forces.
[4]Air Force General Edward Curtis, an old friend of TSL's in-laws.
[5]Gen. Carl "Toohey" Spaatz, commander of the US. Eighth Air Force.
[6]The Cocoanut Grove nightclub fire in Boston on November 29, 1942 killed 300 people. TWL II, at Harvard, was thought to have been in the vicinity of the nightclub at the time of the tragedy.
[7]George Plimpton, son of the New York lawyer Francis Plimpton.

TWL in the same letter repeated a story told at a recent dinner by his cousin, Gardner "Mike" Cowles, the publisher of Look Magazine. Cowles and former Presidential candidate Wendell Willkie had been on a fact-finding trip through China.

Mike and Wendell had been wined and feasted day after day, each banquet surpassing the previous one in variety and length. Mike got along all right until in Chungking he was practically knocked out by creamed shark lips, a rare delicacy that was entirely lost on him. In fact, he had difficulty staying at the table. The following evening there was another great banquet. Course followed course to the number of sixteen. Finally, for dessert, plain vanilla ice cream was served. Mike was so pleased he said to his host, "How nice to have ice cream again!" "Yes," said the host, who was Food Controller for his government, "Early this year we feared a terrible outbreak of cholera. Knowing that milk is the readiest medium for cholera germs, we had to prohibit the manufacture and sale of ice cream entirely. But hearing that Wendell Willkie is so fond of ice cream," he said proudly, "I lifted the embargo this one day just to give it to you fellows."

Christmas 1942 was celebrated at Palisades by FCL and TWL plus a dozen grandchildren and parents. Absent on war duty were TSL in London and their son-in-law, Navy Lieutenant Charles Cunningham.

FCL to TSL
New York City, January 1, 1943

We hung up stockings and talked up the chimney to Santa. After luncheon the grownups gave each other their presents in that blessed breathing spell while the children sleep. My present to each of my children was a genealogical book with the Parmelee[1] coat of arms on the cover.

At five o'clock we had the Christmas tree. That was the best part of the day for me. We all sat in the hall around the lighted tree and sang carols and waited for Santa. Pretty soon we heard his sleigh bells out in the snow. The children's faces were wonderful. Santa rang the doorbell and was admitted by Metcalfe. Santa was Teddy[2] and he did his part superbly. The Gordon Lamonts and Aunt Lillian came for dinner. We had more poems and songs and recitations. Pa and I sang "My Bonnie Lies Over The Ocean" with appropriate gestures. Your health was drunk. After dinner, more presents and the children did a charade, "International". Needless to say, Aunt Margaret suggested the word[3].

TWL to ELC
New York City, January 5, 1943

One of our Paris partners, who has been living at Vichy[4] for over two years and who just escaped from there on the night of November 7th, has now arrived here. He says that the whole Place Vendome in Paris looked for months like a gigantic garage with lorries, lined up on all four sides of the square, being filled up day after day with all the antique furniture from the dealers and residents, museums, etc. It was systematically collected from all Paris and the environs, brought to the Place Vendome for sorting out, then shipped to various points in Germany—alot of it, I suppose, to go into Mr. Goering's various palaces[5].

You know that Mr. Hitler had built at Linz, the birthplace of his mother, the most gigantic museum in the world, occupying several

---

[1]FCL's mother was a Parmelee.

[2]Edward M. Lamont, second son of TSL.

[3]The Third International, organized by the Bolsheviks in 1919, was a network to coordinate the activities of worldwide Communist movements.

[4]The city in occupied France that was the seat of the French government during World War II.

[5]Field Marshal Hermann Goering commanded Hitler's Luftwaffe.

city blocks, for the purpose alone of holding all the loot from Europe. You know, too, that for several years prior to the invasion of Poland in 1939, German professors sent their star pupils into Poland to all the libraries, to the University of Cracow, etc., to get complete lists of all the ancient manuscripts, the products of the monks of the Middle Ages, the incunabula and all that, so that when they made the invasion they were able to work very rapidly and take all these things away, meanwhile destroying all the card catalogues so there would be no way of tracing them.

I am attaching a copy of a few letters I wrote in my first year at Exeter where I started in before I was fourteen . . . Of course, I had no money whatsoever in those days. With my father's salary of $1,000 and with my older brother at Harvard, and my sister at school in Albany, there was just not enough to go around.

A series of letters from FCL to TSL, now 44 and an Army Air Force major in London, reveal FCL's still fiercely mothering instincts, her partiality to the Renaissance mind, and her near obliviousness to the wartime pressures affecting those outside her demesne.

FCL to TSL
New York City, February 3, 1943

Robert Frost, whom I adore, came over for the weekend and there was a great gathering of poets here—Saturday dinner, Sunday luncheon, Sunday tea, Sunday supper, etc. It was great fun and terribly interesting, but of course completely exhausting, as I find most poets like to sit up talking until 2 a.m. I have been in a coma ever since.

Last weekend we had a real blizzard. It was hard getting to Palisades, but once there it was dazzlingly beautiful when the sun came out. It is not a pleasure driving when I go back & forth with milk cans. We bring in enough milk for the week, and as there is an acute milk, cheese and butter shortage, I feel I am performing a civic ser-

Army Air Force Major TSL, 1943

vice. We came in Sunday afternoon and went to Walter Damrosch's 81st birthday party[1]. He takes all the horror of old age away. He is wonderful, the life of every party. We played The Game and I had to act "What's in a Name?" It was a cruel thing to put on me.

Corliss is very seedy. He has not had a vacation for five years and has worked like a maniac.

FCL to TSL
Yeamans Hall, S.C., February 22, 1943

Your fine long letter came. I was interested in every word of it and disagreed with a lot of it. I think it is simply awful to stop all social intercourse and all interests & conversations on things cultural and of the spirit, and to concentrate on military things & on people who are interested only in military affairs. Believe me, you will regret this narrowing of your interests. And what good does it do? "All work and no play makes Jack a dull boy." It is the people who are interested in many things who live with gusto & spirit, who make the greatest contribution.

Look at General Smuts. I have just had a letter from him that takes my breath away. In the midst of his frightful anxieties and cares, he sits down and writes a letter about everything under the sun—wise, witty, inspiring. His letter braced me up, but made me feel like a poor worm with my limited vision and petty thoughts. No, I am convinced you are wrong to concentrate on the war to the exclusion of all else. And I don't believe you do. You just said so to get a rise out of me. But if you really do, you had better take more vitamins. It shows lack of vitality . . .

Why don't you go see H.G. Wells sometime? I had a letter from him yesterday. He would love to see you, he says, and he might be diverting & interesting. He is against DeGaulle, which made me furious.

---

[1] Walter Damrosch, the conductor, composer, and former director of the New York Symphony Orchestra.

Your account of the doctor & dentists you are now patronizing filled me with cold fury. Don't be such a ghastly fool. You'll lose every tooth in your head. It is not worth it. I am amazed at your idiocy. Do you really long so much for a false set in a tumbler of water by your bed?

FCL to TSL
New York City, April 21, 1943

We are all getting ready for the annual Easter Egg hunt at Palisades. There are going to be 12 children and four nurses & governesses and various parents, and every bed in the house taken. It will be rather a slim hunt, as no one is allowed to make chocolate eggs or bunnies anymore . . . . The Woodbridge Memorial lectures[1] started this year, last week in fact. Professor Sheldon of Yale gave the lectures, and I enjoyed them enormously, although I find it exhausting to keep my mind concentrated for 1½ hours. After the last lecture I had all the professors to dinner at my house, also Corliss, also the wives. After dinner we sat in a big group and discussed immortality, free will, Karl Marx, God, evolution and peace. After about an hour, Papa practically crawled under a table and escaped to his bedroom.

TWL has been working hard on the bond issue[2]. He has amazing vitality but looks thin. He never rests. I can't see how he does it all. He is always in a hurry. I think his new responsibilities come rather hard[3].

[1]Named in honor of the late Prof. Frederick Woodbridge, dean of the faculty of Philosophy at Columbia.

[2]As part of a new U.S.-Mexico agreement, which the Morgan bank and TWL had helped negotiate, Mexico was allowed to pay off a portion of its foreign debt via twenty-five year bonds.

[3]TWL had become chairman of the board of his bank, following the death of J.P Morgan, Jr. in March.

TWL to CL
New York City, April 1943

Extract from Mr. Wasson's[1] memorandum of April 29th: " . . . The Russians in Washington continue to be extraordinarily exigent. They will accept only the latest models of machine tools and munitions, and only after the most rigid inspection. They were invited to accept oleomargarine in place of butter, and when they showed reluctance, a blindfold test was staged to prove to them that oleomargarine could not be distinguished from butter. The test was successful. Whereupon the Russians said that since Americans saw no difference between the two, the Americans would have no objection if the Russians would take the butter."

FCL to TSL
New York City, June 8, 1943

I have turned into a mystery woman. I have been ill in bed with temperature for two weeks, and no one has any idea what is the matter with me. It is only a slight temperature. They have tested me for typhoid, para-typhoid, typhus (!), tuberculosis, bad teeth and undulant fever. I have none of them. By the time they got to undulant fever they were desperate—they were determined to have that to pin it on, and almost burst into tears when all tests were negative. All the same, I feel better and I believe the thing is over, whatever it was.

I must try to send you Walter Lippmann's *U.S. Foreign Policy.* It is awfully good. It ought to bring all the flabby, high-falutin idealists (like me) down to earth with a bang.

We talked with Eleanor (ed. ELC) last night. She is completely in love with the West. She has really developed into rather a magnificent creature—big-hearted, generous, courageous, willing to give herself without limit to the people & things she cares about, and awfully efficient—she does big things easily. I sometimes have to do big

---

[1]Gordon Wasson, a Morgan partner and the firm's in-house staff writer.

things, but I do them the hard way. In fact, I am not a bit in love with myself these days. Dearest love to you.

That July, well into his seventies, TWL experienced the first intimations of mortality.

FCL to TSL
North Haven, August, 16, 1943

Father is much better, as I cabled you, and I no longer shiver and shake, but I have been too busy to write.

There are many problems connected with the farm here, none of which I must bother Father with. The mail is enormous. Everyone writing to say how sorry they are to hear, etc., etc. For ten days they would not allow Father to have any mail unless I censored it first, for he must not be emotionally upset.

It started at 5 o'clock Thursday morning with what seemed like a bad heart attack, and was utterly terrifying. I got the local doctor over right away and he did the right thing. Through the day Father was fairly comfortable, but at 9 o'clock that night he had another attack and another one at 10:22. The doctor came over again. He does not inspire confidence. After the last attack he gave me one awful look, then went into the next room and, in plain sight, fell on his knees and began to pray. A little later, I asked him if he thought Father was desperately ill, and he replied, "All we can do now is to trust in Him."

We sat up all night. I managed to get on the telephone, and a Boston specialist, Dr. Ragle, agreed to come up the next day. It was a terrible night of storm. All the lights went out and stayed out. I thought every minute the telephone would go. I do not think the doctor expected Father to live through the night. Saturday morning they took an electric cardiogram which showed no change in his heart for the worse in five years. Dr. Ragle also took a blood count, and after consultation decided it was very bad anemia. The relief at finding it was not a coronary upset was enormous.

From that minute, Pa has gone steadily on, his blood improving all the time. He will probably be allowed to go to the office two hours a day by October 1st. I think he is going to be difficult to manage.

Russell[1] put it very well in a letter: "I hope and pray that hereafter he will conserve his strength for the important things of leadership in public and private life for which he is indispensable, and leave the little things, which he does so well, too, to lesser and younger men. If he will do that, he may still have the years of his greatest usefulness before him. He is a very big man at the height of his powers, and was never more appreciated."

Well, I guess that about finishes it, dear Tommy. I am so very thankful that everything has turned out so well . . . .

TWL to TSL
North Haven, August 31, 1943

Curiously, I did not feel badly or tired until I fell ill. First real illness in 50 years! I have not been allowed to write much. Hence my seeming silence. But here I am on the lawn, looking west to the Camden Hills in the late afternoon sunshine—a three-week succession of those gorgeous Penobscot days. You can see and feel it all . . .

TWL to CL
North Haven, September 1943

I hope you have not continued to overwork by a wide margin, as you usually do. From the age of 14 I have continuously worked very hard for 59 years, which is perhaps as long as a man can normally expect to work at top speed. But unlike you—and most wisely—I have from the time I was 35 insisted on taking long holidays. Generally three months in the summer, not infrequently three weeks in

[1]Russell Leffingwell, another senior Morgan partner, was TWL's closest friend at the bank where both were known as the two "wise men."

winter, sometimes six weeks in spring on semi-business trips abroad. Those are the things that have kept me going hard from 50 years of age on. But if you fail to keep refreshed in the fifteen years before 50, then you feel the strain heavily after that time. Verbum sap!

TWL to ELC
New York City, October 14, 1943

Young Tommy has flunked out of Naval Aviation in Arizona. We all know that the Naval standards are pretty rigid, but are all exceedingly sorry nevertheless. Of course, none of us ever thought he had the slightest aptitude for flying. He has never been able to run a motor car with any degree of assurance. But it is pretty tough. He handled the matter in accordance with his usual practice of never consulting anybody before taking a dramatic step. So he hopped a train to San Diego where there is a big Naval base, and enlisted as a 2d-class seaman. I think he is about as well equipped for that as I should be trying to become a stevedore on the docks of New York.

Regardless, the eldest grandson plunged into boot camp at the San Diego Naval Training Station, then Quartermaster School and, finally, Submarine School. TWL, meanwhile, five months after his attack of "pernicious anemia", suffered a heart attack in December. The family conspired to keep his condition under wraps.

FCL to TSL
New York City, January 18, 1944

This is such a fine chance to get a letter across by Lord H.[1].

I want to tell you more about Father, but he does not want people here to know about the heart complication. I am leery of the Amer-

[1]Lord Halifax, British ambassador to the United States, an old friend and reliable courier in emergencies.

TWL and CL on Penobscot Bay in early 1940s

ican censors, but do not mind the British at all. The thing that distresses me is that, while he is doing really well now, this thing may happen any time—or may not happen for years. But it means that when we go anywhere without a doctor within easy call, we shall have to tote around a trained nurse (if we can get one), and that will be distasteful to Father. Perhaps I can learn to give hypodermics, but I do not at present want that responsibility. I just have to get used to the idea of the sword of Damocles. I am sure I shall learn to live with it quite comfortably. After all, at our age there is so little to lose.

Austin and Corliss have both been perfectly lovely. Austin, on account of his knowledge and tact, has been a tower of strength. Eleanor was here for five days and was sweet and helpful. Ellie & Margaret, too. Eleanor has put on 15 pounds and looks as she did at 15 years, rosy and jolly and pretty. Seattle has done wonders for her. I think I should like to go there to live myself. It would do me good to be bored for a little while.

Did I write you that I had the nicest long letter from J.C.S.[1] all about the Holy Ghost? What an amazing man. In the midst of the war and all the frightful responsibilities & decisions, to write such a letter.

FCL to TSL
Yeamans Hall, S.C., March 10, 1944

Father continues to improve, but everything is different and will never be the same.

This place has become a Naval center, and the noise of airplanes all day and most of the night is simply terrific. TWL doesn't seem to mind it. It drives me to drink. Any sort of sleep is out of the question. Then I think of what you and all my English friends go through all the time, and I am ashamed.

I came down here a sort of wreck because I had a bad fall. I was going out to a dinner party, my first since before Christmas. It was a rainy, windy night and I had on a long dress. As I stepped out of the

[1] Jan Christiaan Smuts.

car, I didn't make the curb and fell flat on the pavement on my face—a terrific crack. I thought of course my nose was broken. My nose bled, my forehead bled, my knees bled. I picked myself up and went into the house, and they wiped me off with some witch hazel and I went to the dinner looking like an old witch and sat between John Erskine[1] and Stark Young[2] and had a wonderful time until I felt ill and went home.

Next day I had all sorts of X-rays taken. Nothing was broken. The X-ray doctor came into the room where I was sitting. He was cross about something and said over his shoulder to someone in his office, "That's the stupidest thing I ever saw." "Oh, no, doctor," said I, "the stupidest thing you ever saw is sitting on this bench."

TWL to CL
Yeamans Hall, March 26, 1944

I am glad that, with your arm better and a brief three weeks of change, life seems to be more cheerful again. As for myself, despite wars and cruelties and confusion incredible, I am glad to be living at this hour. If I had to choose, I should choose no other day nor generation. *This* is the time to be alive!

TWL to TSL
New York City, April 12, 1944

I have been starting in on very short hours at the office and expect to take it very easily. My trouble has seemed to be, all my life, there was no human thermostat that had been invented to register any degree of fatigue I might have. In other words, unlike your mother, I don't get a feeling of being terribly tired or exhausted, so consequently, without knowing it, I just seem to crack now and then.

---

[1] Prof. John Erskine, educator, author, and concert pianist who became president of the Juillard School of Music.
[2] Stark Young, American journalist, playwright, poet and drama critic.

FCL to TSL
New York City, April 15, 1944

Yesterday was your wedding anniversary, so I went over to see Ellie and she read me a letter you had written Elinor[1] about reading to some little girls during an air raid. I must say, spending one's nights in a cellar does not appeal to me a bit, and I do not see how you can do your work the next day. In fact, I think we in America have not any idea of how hard life is in other countries. Everybody is living very much as usual, buying spring clothes, going to concerts and theaters. Of course, people work at the Red Cross, etc., but the pattern of life has changed very little.

We had Col. Astor[2] of *The Times* to tea the other day. He always leaves me as he finds me. Russell[3] came, too, and we had our never-ending argument and disagreement about the kind of peace we want, I mean the kind of international organization. Russell and TWL always say, "But, my dear (meaning, my poor dear little idiot), America would never stand for that." She wouldn't? Well, then, she'll go on sacrificing her sons & daughters every 25 years. We have got to have a much more radical change than they envisage.

I have just finished Anne Morrow's[4] book. Her last two books have made me dislike C[5] intensely, the last thing she intended to do. It is beautiful in places and rather exalted & very poetic in quality. I think she lives on a higher plane than most people. (That sounds like a bad joke but wasn't meant to be.) I feel it every time I talk to her. I suppose that is greatly to be desired, to hold yourself at your best and highest—but so awfully hard.

[1]Elinor Lamont, the eight-year-old daughter of the TSLs.
[2]John Jacob Astor, a principal owner of *The Times* of London.
[3]Russell Leffingwell.
[4]Anne Morrow Lindbergh.
[5]Charles Lindbergh.

TWL to TWL II
New York City, May 18, 1944

Old Mr. Henry Ford was in to see me yesterday. He is a great character, eighty-one years old but lively as a cricket. Comes in to see us a couple of times a year[1]. Never wears a hat. I was recalling to him how he had, with his Model T, revolutionized the life of the American people, making accessible to almost everybody any part of the country. Then I asked him whether, when he was a young man just starting in on his Model T, he had in the back of his mind a dream like this that might come true. He said, no, he did not. He was just terribly interested in machinery and in the possibilities of a gasoline engine.

Even in his twilight years TWL remained remarkably clear-eyed about the realities of power and the constraints of idealism.

TWL to TSL
New York City, May 25, 1944

Thank you ever so much for your comments on my letter in the Sunday *Times.* I may well have grown to be one of those tired old men with complete loss of ideals, but I am not quite ready to admit it yet.

You see, what burned me up in Paris in 1919 was that President Wilson did not let the Conference[2] get down to any concrete propositions except the League of Nations. Meantime, European conditions were deteriorating all over the Continent. There was fighting

[1]Henry Ford was customarily no admirer of Wall Street financiers, but he had patronized TWL's bank ever since the Pecora hearings in 1933. J.P. Morgan Jr.'s unruffled testimony before the Senators, his equanimity over the midget-in-his-lap episode, had greatly impressed Ford.

[2]The post-World War I peace conference in which TWL participated.

in Russia; there was fighting in Hungary. In lots of different places questions that might have been comparatively easy of solution, if they had been tackled immediately, were allowed to go from bad to worse. That is what's in the back of my mind. It is not at all to discourage for a moment future plans for world organization. I say in my letter that we have got to take part in such an organization, but that the blueprints for it at the moment are not as important as more immediate problems . . .

There are burning post-war questions we are facing now: that of stabilizing currencies so we can be assured of a sound basis for world trade. We shan't have a peaceful world unless we can re-establish world trade. None of these thousands of good professors working here over world organization blueprints seem to give a darn about the importance of having, as a partner in any future organization, a strong Britain—and what steps we could take, useful to ourselves and to Britain, along that line. It is easy enough to take the word 'empirical' and ridicule it, but I don't know that any of the biggest things in this world were ever arrived at by a purely preliminary theoretical blueprint.

As to the old League of Nations, yes, of course it was the weakness of man that made it a failure . . . the weakness of Mr. Wilson as a human being that he failed to allow a Covenant to be drawn up that was workable. No country—America, Britain, or any other—is going to bind itself to take action fifteen years hence under a set of circumstances that we attempt to describe today . . . The world seemed to assume that the League would work when it was based on the false premise that the world could avoid war by not wanting it, and by disarming and ostracizing the bad countries economically and otherwise, and by forming a league of forty or fifty nations to discuss and debate things, when only half a dozen of them were disposed of the military and industrial power to do anything about it. The separation of power and authority was one of the fatal things about the League.

We shall never get anywhere until the nonsensical notion of the equality of sovereign states is discarded. Only the great powers who have to fight the wars can settle the policies which prevent them . . .

TWL II set sail from San Diego that June aboard the submarine Snook, *bound for enemy waters in the far Pacific. He left behind a girl. His last words written to her: " . . . These weeks, snatched with a smile and tear from the great, cruel, befuddled rush of war, have been the happiest in my life. But why should I be sad when the very thought of you is a treasure few men find? I love you, darling, on and on into the stars which have no end."*

Still another leave-taking clouded the Lamonts' lives.

TWL to ELC
New York City, June 3, 1944

Last week, Thursday, your mother sent Metcalfe off for his holiday. He went home as usual. Yesterday morning, Friday, his wife called up to say he had collapsed. He had a hemorrhage, and the doctor thought it was probably some stomach ulcer. But the heart was also affected. He was rushed to the New Rochelle Hospital. Austin had come to town for the day, so he went right up after luncheon. Metcalfe was in an oxygen tent. He looked badly, but the doctor said he wasn't in too bad shape. Suddenly, however, at 4:30 he simply stopped breathing and was gone. You know what a horrible blow this is. Metcalfe was so much a part of us all that it is like losing a member of the family.

FCL to TSL
North Haven, July 2, 1944

Metcalfe's death was the most awful shock to me, and grief. Father and I feel we have lost our best friend and most devoted. Outside my immediate family, children, grandchildren, there is no one whose death would have been such a loss to me, not a single friend. Father took M's death very calmly. We did not let him go to the funeral or see Metcalfe. I went out to Mt. Vernon the day before the funeral and saw Metcalfe. He really looked quite beautiful & very noble . . .

ELC

Later that June, TWL and FCL had traveled to Cambridge, Mass., where TWL was honored with Harvard's Alumni Medal for Distinguished Service. Walter Lippmann received an honorary degree. FCL, continuing her letter to TSL, took note of her sharp differences with TWL on how the post-war peace should be organized. In no way did she share TWL's reservations about the "equality of sovereign states" under an international structure like the United Nations.

Father and I went up to Harvard Commencement. It was not only a hot day, but the hottest I ever remember. Pa stood it very well. He did not sit on the platform with the other elder statesmen, but under a tree, and that saved his life . . . I insisted, alone, on clapping all the parts of Walter Lippmann's speech dealing with an international organization. After I had clapped alone three times, the whole audience began to clap.

Father and I are not of one mind about organizing for peace after the war. I think it should be done *now* as far as possible. Here we are, all working together, all feeling that no price is too great to pay for peace; at least, every woman feels that. (You talk to a woman who has a son in the war about 'national interests', and she laughs in your face; she wants freedom from war, and sovereignty be damned.)

We ought to get some good solid peace organization going while this longing runs high. And it can't be done piecemeal or by trial & error. We've got to take some chances. Of course, the Big Three[1] will be the central core, but they are more likely to stick together if they are part of some well thought-out organization like the United Nations, some going concern. Otherwise they may drift apart.

Some people say, "But we don't want any committee bossing our country." Well, who forced our country into war this time? Japan did, by attacking us. We had no choice. I should much prefer to have a committee of high-minded democratic nations helping us make de-

[1]Britain, Russia and the United States.

cisions than to leave it to the decisions of Germany, Japan, or any barbaric state that chooses to force us into war. I think Russell[1] and TWL have a rather old men's point of view about after the war.

TWL to CL
North Haven, July 18, 1944

Life goes on here much as if there were no war, except for the lack of gasoline and hired help. The weather has been gorgeous, but no rain and the fields are drying up . . . Tommy is in France, we believe.[2]

The other day a scow, loaded with a shattered blimp, came down from Northeast and went through the Thoroughfare[3]. At the same time, Paul Cabot[4] blew in on a cruise from N.E. and declared that a German submarine had shot down the blimp and killed two of our men.

FCL to TSL
North Haven, July 24, 1944

Your letter to Ellie came. It gave me the best idea I had had about the buzz bombs[5]. I am glad you have left them, but I can't help worrying over Normandy. You know you are just too old, and there's no

---

[1]Russell Leffingwell.

[2]TSL, now a Lieutenant Colonel, had been assigned to new headquarters in Normandy a few weeks after the D-day invasion.

[3]Northeast Harbor; the Thoroughfare between North Haven and Vinalhaven.

[4]Paul Cabot, a prominent Bostonian, pioneer in mutual funds, and TSL's close friend. Cabot, who had also met FDR on one of his stopovers in Pulpit Harbor, took the President up on his word to call on him at the White House the next time Cabot was in Washington. Undeterred when FDR's secretary told him the President was too busy to see him for several hours, Cabot breezed past her into the Oval Office. He reminded FDR of their meeting on the *Potomac* in Pulpit, said he would take only a minute of FDR's time, and got right to the point. Mr. President, Cabot said, your Secretary of the Treasury is about to do a terrible thing by taxing mutual funds. FDR smiled, shook his head and assured Cabot no such thing would happen. And it didn't.

[5]Hitler's pilotless, buzzing V-1 rockets had killed thousands of Londoners and other Britons.

getting around it, for that sort of thing—sleeping on the ground in a bag, and nothing but a pup tent over you . . . not good for your old bones. And the news keeps coming of torrential downpours in Normandy. The account of your practicing putting up the pup tent in St. James Park gave me my first good laugh in weeks. All the same, I can't help being worried about you.

The news is terribly exciting about the revolt in Germany[1]. I think Friday was the most exciting day of the war—except perhaps D-day. I was in a state of cold fury all day because from 9:30 a.m until 10 p.m. every single radio station gave nothing but the news of the Democratic Convention, hour after hour, these nasal, vapid voices pouring out eulogies for some favorite son. Let empires rise & fall, but don't miss one word of some d—— fool in Nebraska nominating some other d—— fool for the vice-presidency[2].

All your family came to luncheon yesterday, Sunday, and we all went to church. We now fill nearly three pews, and when the Corliss Lamonts get here we shall practically fill the church. Julian C[3] continues to pass the plate like a German sergeant, only his coat always rumples up the back. Pa continues to make the natives' eyes stick out by tossing in ten-dollar bills . . .

FCL to TSL
North Haven, August 14, 1944

. . . The Corliss Lamont children are here in Eleanor's house. I insisted on their all going to church. I hope to save their souls.

---

[1]The failed bombing assassination attempt on Hitler that week, by a cabal of army officers, confirmed a serious rift in the German military.

[2]The "other d—— fool" turned out to be Sen. Harry S. Truman who was nominated to join FDR on the Democratic ticket that July.

[3]Dr. Julian Coolidge, a distinguished Harvard professor whose family summered on North Haven.

Over the next eight months the volume of letters to their children tailed off. The war in Europe was racing to conclusion. TSL had returned from Europe to civilian life. TWL's health continued its slow decline. FCL was distracted.

In April 1945, TWL wrote a long anecdotal letter to his two eldest grandsons in which he recounted a story about the great Soviet general, Georgi Zhukov. Marshal Zhukov—defender of Stalingrad, savior of Leningrad, now commanding all Russian forces in the final assault on Berlin—had once worked as lowly office boy in a British oil firm in the Caucasus. Old colleagues, it seemed, remembered Zhukov as "idle, lazy, slothful, impudent," a boy who "never did a lick of work and was simply useless." TWL observed: "This whole episode only goes to show that it doesn't do to attempt to judge a man too early in life. He may have in him the elements of greatness."

The letter concluded: "We haven't heard from you for a long time, Tommy. I do hope we shall soon. Let us know how you are. Lots of love from Grandpa."

TWL II probably never received the letter. Earlier that month the Snook, *heading for Formosan waters on its ninth war patrol, had radioed her position to a fellow ship. It was the last anyone heard of her. On May 14, one week after Germany's surrender, the Navy Department telegram reached TWL II's family. It reported him missing in action. The news not only devastated his parents, it came as a particularly cruel blow to TWL and FCL who had put such store in their promising first grandchild.*

It was weeks before they could summon up the old wit and badinage when their letters resumed.

TWL to AL
New York City, June 5, 1945

Everybody about town is talking hormones. I don't mean for the purpose of stimulating sex virility, but just for stepping up old age in general. The town and press seem quite excited over them. What is the matter with your turning up a few (cd. hormone tablets) to put me back at least into the 60's if I can't go further!

FCL to AL
North Haven, July 20, 1945

You are doing important work, you are working to heal people, to make them whole again. That is really the work of the divine creative spirit, and when you have a partnership like that you are helped & sustained & invigorated . . .

P.S. Have you heard this one? The Senate fiddles while Byrnes roams.[1] .

The surrender of Japan that August ended six years of global warfare on an unprecedented scale. Even as it marked the coming of the atomic age, it also wrote finis to the old order. Many women, accustomed to their newfound self-reliance as workers on the war front, forsook their old domestic ways for independent careers. The changes would affect the manorial lifestyles of the rich.

TWL to TSL
New York City, October 11, 1945

Please give this with my love to Ned Miner[2] as indicating domestic household conditions in this country and in England:

> The King was in the laundry a-washin' out a shirt,
> The Queen was in the kitchen a-sweepin' up the dirt,
> The maid was in the parlor eating bread and honey,
> In came a neighbor and offered her more money.

[1]James Byrnes, the peripatetic Secretary of State, was off again on yet another diplomatic mission, this time to the Potsdam Conference in Berlin.
[2]Edward G. Miner, TSL's father-in-law.

FCL to AL
Gasparilla Inn, Boca Grande, Florida, January 1946

The trip down beggars description. We reached Tampa two hours late. The plane was like an igloo. Miss D——[1] and I had on fur coats, sweaters, woolen panties and an extra coat over our knees. For six hours my teeth chattered. We reached Tampa at 8 p.m. and had to get a bite to fortify us for the 100-mile auto ride. We went to a Spanish restaurant and all they had ready was a black bean soup à la onions & rice. The onions were raw, so was the rice, and the beans not cooked much either. We ate ravenously and for the next 12 hours had horrible stomach aches. That helped pass the time.

The motor car driver did not know the road. There was a detour and we never got back on the main road. We stopped and asked the way frequently. About 12 o'clock I asked if we were not nearly at Boca Grande and the driver said, "Yes, nearly to Placida." I said, "Why Placida?" He said, "Oh, that's where you leave the auto and take a little boat to Boca Grande." I said, "Does the boat run after midnight?" He said, "I dunno, it's doubtful." That was my blackest moment. We went on board a miserable little boat, transferred our baggage, and set out to sea. We reached Gasparilla at 1:00 a.m.

FCL to CL
Boca Grande, Florida, February 1946

I spend hours a day reading of the terrible state of the world. In two days I have forgotten most of it and get Walter Lippmann & *Times* editorials & William Shirer[2] and the Alsop brothers[3] all mixed up. It is quite amusing to be losing your mind. I enjoy it . . .

---

[1]Miss Dahl, TWL's private nurse.
[2]William L. Shirer, the journalist and author of *Berlin Diary*.
[3]Joseph and Stewart Alsop, the Washington political columnists.

AL in his early forties

AL to TWL
Torrey Cliff, September 2, 1946

My experience with sick people has given me some insight into the mental agonies which an illness such as yours inevitably brings, and into the way patients in your position usually react. The true quality of a man is often revealed when he attains great success in the world such as you have; and the world knows how you have met that test. But even more revealing, I think, is the manner in which a man meets great adversity of which he has had no previous experience and against which he cannot fight. That is what you have faced these last three years & especially these last three months. I say that nothing you have ever done is as fine or as brave as your handling of this insidious adversary. In this, as in everything else, you have set us the highest standard.

With much love,
Austin

TSL to CL
New York City, January 28, 1947

For some time Father has been very much interested in the possibility of making a gift for the rebuilding and restoring of one of the great cathedrals of England damaged by German bombing during the war. He has considered taking this action not only because some of the great historic edifices of England are in desperate need if they are to be preserved, but because the making of such a gift would probably strengthen goodwill between England and America. It would be a happy symbol of Anglo-American friendship, meeting approval on both sides of the Atlantic. You can realize, knowing Father's wide circle of friendships in Great Britain, how this idea has had an especial appeal to him. He has now made up his mind to make a gift of $500,000 for the restoration of Canterbury Cathedral.

FCL to AL
Boca Grande, Florida, January 19, 1947

It is as beautiful as I dreamed it would be. Father stood the trip well, and is fairly well now, but not very. He seems to me increasingly weak . . .

I will now state that I have never worked harder in my life than this last week. Everything went wrong. The gas stove did something queer, and the cook's hair caught fire and her eyebrows were burned off. The refrigerator has not come and the weather is very hot. There is a pump right under the servants' rooms that makes the most nerve-wracking & loud noise all night long. They cannot sleep. The water has gone brackish so that if you water the plants, they die. And if you *don't* water them, they die. You can't get any workmen to do anything. Last night I was up from 1:00 to 2:00 a.m. trying to fix some pipes in Pa's bathroom that began making a noise like a ship at sea blowing a fog horn. I fixed the pipes and the noise stopped. I'll bet you never knew I was a master plumber. Well, I am.

My blood pressure is as high as ever. Poor old Father is very deaf. I forgot to say how restful & luxurious the trip down was. I had a temperature of over 100° and went to bed & stayed there & had a most delightful time.

TWL to CL
Boca Grande, Florida, March 26, 1947

Hearty congratulations upon the turn of the year for you! I can very well remember your first birthday in a little house we occupied on Thomas Street in Englewood, now called Sherwood Place. You have moved a long distance from those days—in fact, all of us have.

CL in his early forties

FCL to CL
Boca Grande, Florida, March 28, 1947

Many happy returns of the day. You are a great comfort to your old Ma, and I take enormous pride in you, in your mind and character and attainments. I wish you could believe in Comrade God as part of this beautiful and mysterious universe. Then I should be quite happy . . .

FCL to CL
Boca Grande, Florida, January 1948

Father is desperately ill. I do not think the doctor expects him to pull up, but he hopes he will. I feel so alone. It is rather silly of you to say, "Alone? Why you have the radio, the telephone and the newspapers." Do call me up once in a while. And don't be so intellectual that you lose your humanity and the overflowing affection you were born with. It is very cold here . . .

The sun is out at last and it is warmer. Perhaps things will turn for the better. Pa is too weak to talk. All I can do is sit by him and hold his hand and pray for him. He seems to like to have me there.

TWL died on February 2, 1948 in Boca Grande. He was 77 and, in keeping with his style, he went peacefully.

His lifespan had embraced an early sighting of the Queen who gave her name to the Victorian era and, a half-century later, the fiery debut of the atomic age. A thousand people filled the church in New York for his services. Twenty years earlier, while steaming up the Nile with FCL, TWL had written CL: "Funerals are, I suppose, a survival of pagan rites; yet, just as they have lasted for thousands of years, so they will endure for centuries to come. They furnish the only chance for friends to show their last need of respect and affection. It is not for the dead person. He has achieved his victory and his peace; it is for the living."

The Reverend Thomas Lamont, TWL's father, had earned less than $1,200 a year as a village parson in the late 1800s, and somehow raised a family on it. The young TWL, a newspaper columnist noted upon his death, had "had to pinch pennies, his only advantage being a spiritual home, a zeal for work and a belief in himself." But like his father, who tithed his income for charity, TWL had never flagged in his habit of giving throughout his life. He, too, tithed his income for good works, and gave abundantly to friends and colleagues in need. Thus, at his death, the remarkable scale of his bequests—from gifts to the islanders of his beloved North Haven to the building of a great library that would benefit future generations of Harvard undergraduates.

The boy who grew up poor in a Methodist parsonage, four centuries after the completion of Canterbury Cathedral's nave, honored his pledge to repair the wounds inflicted by the Luftwaffe and the natural ravages of age. The words by John Masefield on a tablet in the cathedral's great cloister, dedicated to both TWL and FCL, lauded his special generosity: "All lovely giving is a Heavenly seed/Dropped to the chosen heart as glittering corn/That everlasting gladness may be born/Bread never spent, Beauty that never ends."

FCL to AL
New York City, February 24, 1948

Happy birthday to you. You have been a pillar of strength and sustaining love to your father & mother these last four and a half years. Your presence and care meant so much to Father. I really do not believe I could have lived without you, or carried my burdens at all. May God bless you.

FCL to CL
R.M.S. Queen Elizabeth, Spring 1948

We are nearly over and have lost the sun as we approach England. I am much rested. My only problem is to resist the temptation of spending all my time in a hot salt bath, which for me is the third pleasantest thing in life: 1. Getting a new idea, 2. Falling in love, 3. A hot salt bath . . .

FCL to AL
Hyde Park Hotel, London, June 28, 1948

I *long* to get home. I have seen the Toynbees[1], Cliveden, Walter de la Mare, Lady Colefax, Harold Nicholson[2], St. John and Nora Ervine, Lady St. Just (Florrie Grenfell), the Murrays, General Smuts, the Halifaxes (tomorrow), dinner with the Huxleys the night before I sail . . . I am homesick and wish I were sailing tomorrow in spite of all the interesting people.

FCL to CL
Hyde Park Hotel, London, July 1948

My friends are perfectly lovely to me. I had a restful and pleasant visit with the Masefields . . . I have just come back from Cliveden. General Wavell[3] was there, silent as the grave. The whole atmosphere was very conservative and roused all the rebel in me, and I didn't have sense enough to keep my mouth shut. Of course, politically we are miles apart, and about Russia, too, and they all, including the guests, approved of flogging in the public schools. After my eloquent plea against it, Gen. Wavell addressed the only remark he made to me during the entire weekend, which was, "I hope it goes on for a long time."

FCL to CL
North Haven, Summer 1948

I am sitting out on the grass looking off to the Camden Hills on a most beautiful day, with masses of soft white clouds drifting by. I went to church this morning and it was hard for me. Everyone came

---

[1]Arnold Toynbee, the Oxford historian and author of the monumental *Study of History.*

[2]Harold Nicholson, the biographer, historian and diplomat, married to Vita Sackville-West, the novelist.

[3]Field Marshal Archibald Wavell, supreme commander of Allied forces in the Middle and Far East in World War II.

up and spoke to me and was very sweet. The clergyman looked like an old monk painted in a missal, and his sermon was in keeping. Oh, Cor, why aren't you in the church to bring a fresh flow of ideas to it? I have not given up hope yet.

FCL to CL
Florida, February 23, 1949

I have had a very miserable time the last week or ten days. Something happened to my back. Have you ever seen a beetle lying on its back, waving its legs futilely in the air? That's what happened to me.

FCL to CL
Florida, March 24, 1949

I have finished your book[1], all but the last chapter. It ought to have a great success. It is so alive and so far from the wordy, rigid, pessimistic philosophy of these modern days. It discusses everything from Wordsworth's poetry to the possibility of colonizing Mars. It is a pity that quite a bit of it is given over to flogging a dead horse. It is a criticism of your mother & upbringing that you do not seem to have much idea of what liberal Christianity stands for.

FCL to AL
Wilbury Park, Nr Salisbury, June 18, 1950

I think I am getting a bit too old & tired for travel.

Corliss, Margaret, Margot, Hayes, Florence and Anne (ed. the entire CL family) have just this minute left after a hearty tea to which they did full justice. They are going to a London hotel which does not seem to exist. It is in neither the telephone book or in a city directory. Corliss does not know the address.

I have seen almost everybody—Gilbert M[2], looking very ill; John Masefield, decidedly better than last year, and Constance who can't

---

[1]CL's *Humanism as a Philosophy*, New York; Philosophical Library.
[2]Gilbert Murray.

bear to let him out of her sight for a minute, and I do not blame her. She is deafer than ever . . . Philip and Irene Noel-Baker, the Cecils, the Toynbees, Walter de la Mare . . . these all represent lunches. If they give me a choice, I always choose luncheon instead of dinner. It's less tiring.

When I came over, all fussed up about Senator McCarthy[1], it was refreshing to spend the afternoon with de la Mare and discuss whether trees have consciousness . . .

FCL to CL
North Haven, August 5, 1950

I was greatly troubled by your statement to the National Committee of the Progressive Party. You do not seem to realize that the United States is now at war—under the United Nations, to be sure, but it is still at war, and things that are all right to say in time of peace just will not go down in wartime.[2]. Paul Robeson[3] had just had his passport voided, and you cannot expect calm and cool judgment when your country is at war. Of course, you may think that the best way to serve your country is to spend the duration of the war in prison, but I cannot agree . . .

I don't know what you mean by "American intervention in Korea under the mantle of United Nations action." Do you no longer believe in the United Nations? . . . You don't say a word about the Soviets' increase of armaments, although the reason we are having such a hard time in Korea is that we did not increase armaments enough. How about the Soviets fanning anti-American hysteria not only in Russian and the satellite nations, but throughout the world? You

---

[1]Sen. Joseph McCarthy (R-Wis.) had launched his campaign against alleged Communists in the federal government earlier that year.

[2]North Korea had invaded South Korea in June, precipitating the U.N. 'police action' that became the Korean War. CL vehemently opposed the massive U.S. involvement in the conflict.

[3]Paul Robeson, the celebrated actor and bass singer, had ignited controversy as an outspoken Communist sympathizer. CL was equally enraged that Robeson's passport had been lifted, a penalty he himself would experience.

know that I am no friend of war and that my feeling against military action is almost an obsession with me. But I cannot see how the United Nations could take this aggression and defiance of its orders without doing something about it.

. . . My toe is not any better and Austin suggests cutting it off.

FCL to CL
North Haven, August 28, 1951

You have been an angel to write me so often and to send me all the books and articles. I do appreciate it even if I haven't written and said so. I think *The Independent Mind* came out very well, and I congratulate you[1].

. . . I know I ought to get out in the fog and take a little walk, because the doctors have said so, and I go and the next thing I know it is lunch time, and no letter for Corliss. Afternoons I sleep . . .

Two decades earlier, in one of her letters, FCL had raged against the dying light, emphatically warning her sons that there was "no twilight about me" and that she would "never spend my days in a cemetery." But the twilight deepened over the coming year, 1952, and four days after Christmas FCL died in New York at the age of eighty.

That fall, in absentia, she may have cast her last presidential vote. For, as one columnist recalled at her passing, FCL had recently joked, "I'm the only one in America who voted for General Eisenhower and Corliss Lamont."[2]. Like TWL, she was greathearted in her bequests, most of which went to a half-dozen or more leading women's colleges. It was the abundance and quality of her spirit, however, that her children and friends remembered. In The Times of London, the Masefields recalled

[1] *The Independent Mind: Essays of a Humanist Philosopher,* by CL.

[2] CL at various times ran for office as the candidate of the American Labor Party or the Independent Socialist Party.

that, "There was in her look and bearing such a spirit of gaiety, life and wisdom, that none who knew her will ever think of her as dead."

In the end, though she still haunted a family Christmas or two, FCL had to settle for a cemetery plot across the Hudson, a patch of green beside TWL, only a few paces from her children who would follow her there over the decades to come. From time to time, it's said, she still offers them her frank advice.

Acknowledgments

The letters whose excerpts are quoted at length in this book were originally assembled in the early 1960s by the late Frances Van Schaick of Richmondville, New York, at the request of my father. She labeled them, whimsically, "Yr Everloving Ma and Da: Letters to Their Children from Florence C. and Thomas W. Lamont." They spanned a period from 1913 to 1952. I am indebted to Miss Van Schaick and to her nephew-in-law Graeme Bell who made the letters available to me.

They were also made available to my brother Edward Lamont who used many of them in a different context for his excellent biography of our grandfather and his career, *The Ambassador from Wall Street* (Madison Books, 1994). That book served as a useful reference guide in corroborating the background of a number of these letters, and I am grateful to the author.

Three other fine source books which provided insight on the era these letters cover are *The House of Morgan* by Ron Chernow (Atlantic Monthly Press, 1990); *Promised Land, Crusader State* by Walter McDougall (Houghton Mifflin, 1997); and *The Thomas Lamont Family,* edited by Corliss Lamont (Horizon Press, New York, 1962).

I particularly thank my friend Tom Wallace whose helpful suggestions and interest in this project bore as always the marks of a discerning literary agent. I also blow appreciative kisses to my beloved wife Ada who garners no twilight about her, either.

Finally, I'm ever so obliged to my cousins Margaret Lamont Heap, Lavinia Lamont Rosenthal and Priscilla Cunningham for taking the time and trouble to rummage through their family albums in search of the telling photograph to meet the editor's special requests. Top-grade sleuths, all of them!

No Twilight About Me has been computer typeset in Columbus MT, a typeface designed by Patricia Sanders at the Monotype Type Drawing Office in 1992 to celebrate the quincentenary of the voyage from Spanish shores by Christopher Columbus. The roman weight is based on types used in Spain by Jorge Coci circa 1513, probably originating from Italy and traveling via France. The italic is derived from a font cut by Rober Franjon circa 1543 and used by Bartolemé de Najéra in 1548 to print a famous manual by the writing master Juan de Yciar.

Design and production services by Martin Cook Associates, Ltd.